Colliding with Destiny

Colliding with Destiny

FINDING HOPE IN THE LEGACY OF RUTH

SARAH JAKES

BETHANYHOUSE

a division of Baker Publishing Group
Minneapolis, Minnesota

© 2013, 2014 by Sarah D. Jakes, LLC

The 2014 edition is expanded from the 2013 edition

Published by Bethany House Publishers
11400 Hampshire Avenue South
Bloomington, Minnesota 55438
www.bethanyhouse.com

Bethany House Publishers is a division of
Baker Publishing Group, Grand Rapids, Michigan

Printed in the United States of America

Library of Congress Cataloging-in-Publication Data
Jakes, Sarah.
    Colliding with destiny : finding hope in the legacy of Ruth / Sarah Jakes.
       pages cm
    Summary: "Sarah Jakes uses the biblical book of Ruth to show women how the most painful times in life can be the most pivotal, propelling them into a destiny they'd never imagined"— Provided by publisher.
       ISBN 978-0-7642-1211-6 (cloth : alk. paper)
       ISBN 978-0-7642-1289-5 (international trade paper : alk. paper)
       1. Bible. Ruth—Devotional literature. I. Title.
    BS1315.54.J35 2014
    222'.3506—dc23   2014017426

Cover design by LOOK Design Studio

Author is represented by Dupree/Miller & Associates

14 15 16 17 18 19 20   7 6 5 4 3 2 1

Because I needed to believe I wasn't alone,
I found a woman who went ahead of us all
and showed that grace survives
our most broken moments.

Contents

Contents

Introduction

Now that we're adults, my brother and I have created this new tradition. Whenever we stay at my parents' home, we take the opportunity to spend some quality time together. He loves being an uncle to my kids, and I love for them to get to know him. So after the kids have finished their homework, had supper, and taken their baths, we all settle in to relax together. Whether it's watching something on television, spending time talking about each other's day, dancing around to music, or play fighting, we always have fun.

Sometimes we even turn our hanging out into a team sport! Yes, the girls versus the boys, sibling teams versus sibling teams, or school versus school. Everything except for the play fights—that comes down to Malachi, my son, and Dexter, my brother. I just commentate or instigate, proving an important role in the morale of the fight.

One evening recently, we were trying to teach Malachi the art of boxing. Dexter and I would emulate the proper stance, bounce, and posture. But we also stressed the most important factors:

heart and attitude. Turning the family room into a makeshift boxing ring, we all burst into laughter as my six-foot-four little brother and five-foot-three son playfully squared off. Imitating Floyd Mayweather and Muhammad Ali, they both turned it all the way on!

After they engaged in this lighthearted contest, I again tried to show Malachi a boxer's stance. At ten years old, he had never seen an actual fight, so he had no clue what to do.

"Watch this," I said and gave my best Laila Ali impression. *Bounce, bounce. Bob, weave. Uppercut. Jab, jab. Bounce. Weave.* My son, timid in nature, looked up at me with wide eyes.

"But, Mom, I can't even reach his face!" he exclaimed.

I looked at him and smiled. But before I opened my mouth to reply, I heard, "I CAN REACH HIS FACE, MAMA!"

I looked down at my three-year-old, three-foot-high daughter, Makenzie. In perfect Laila Ali stance, down to the rhythm of her bounce, Makenzie was prepared to take on Dex. She had been watching us the whole time. Never recognizing their differences in size, she was ready to face the challenge.

Makenzie had no concept of how much smaller she was in comparison to her competition. All she knew was that she had the heart to fight the battle. It didn't occur to her to be intimidated by someone bigger.

What if we dared to believe with the heart of a child?

Somewhere along the path of life, we start to size up the competition. We start to look at how big the challenge before us is and get discouraged. Little by little, the punches of life begin to bruise our hope. We stop fighting as hard as we once did because we don't believe we can win anymore. We don't block very well because we're expecting the knockout that will end it all. We stop living, out of fear.

Fear is the most shameful ghost of them all. Painful memories of past fights convince us that some things are not worth the risk of fighting at all. We allow our past to dictate our every move. We stand in place and wait for life to hit us again.

Certainly we're taught to always keep the faith. But when life's blows rock us to our core, it's hard to remember that our pain has a purpose. When the aches of what happened, what should have happened, and what could have happened haunt our every decision, keeping the faith can be a challenge.

If disappointments have kept you from being your true self, then this book is for you. My friend, please allow me to share with you the story of Ruth—*all of her story*, not just the happy ending. We often hear of Ruth having her Boaz, but we rarely discuss the collisions she faced on the road to her destiny. While it's imperative that we remember her legacy, we can only give it value if we see the price she paid for it.

Could it be that if you dare to live again, your story doesn't have to be associated with what broke you? That by doing whatever it takes to survive, you will sow seeds of redemption into your future?

Ruth's story begins with her being an outcast. Shunned in her homeland of Moab because she left the religion of the land and embraced her husband's beliefs, Ruth remained committed to her new husband and new God. And then again, when she returned to her mother-in-law's hometown, Bethlehem, she was shunned for being a foreigner from a pagan land. She carried the burdens of both who she was and who she used to be.

When Ruth worshiped with her husband's family in her hometown, there was a religious differentiation that caused her to be an outcast. She no longer bowed to their idols or prayed to their false gods. In Bethlehem, she was talked about because of her mystery. It was what people didn't know about her that intrigued them the most. She seemed like them, but on the inside she was not the same.

Ruth knew that sometimes it's our silent heartaches, the ones that bring tears to our eyes and make us want to drown the pain, that often separate us from others. But she also knew the faithfulness of her Lord, the ways He transformed her pain into His perfection. The trials that Ruth endured on the way to her collision with destiny offer hope to each of us. Whether what has broken you can be seen by the world or is a silent burden you whisper in your pillowcase at night, God can still use your struggle to propel you to your destiny!

Ruth's story has inspired me to share this book with you to help aid you on your journey of colliding with divine destiny. It is my prayer that it will release clues from God that lead you back to Him like never before. It is my hope that your spirit will be refreshed, uplifted, and upheld as you move forward to the treasure that awaits you.

While studying the book of Ruth, I was reminded that God can restore life's most damaging collisions. In my time with Ruth, I learned that survival is so much more than a perky smile and dozens of friends. It's more than pretending to have it all together on the outside. Survival just means you do what you can with what you have left. And trust that God will do the rest.

Whether your heart has been broken because love had a devastating ending for you or your body has been ravaged by a painful disease, this book is for you. Or maybe you have a past you feel you can't escape. Maybe you're trying to reinvent yourself after life has dealt you its hardest blow. Maybe each day is an excruciating battle with depression. Maybe you're surrounded by other people while suffering the inner loneliness of not belonging. No matter what it is, you *will* have something in common with Ruth.

Imagine yourself being free. Bright-eyed, three-year-old Makenzie/Laila Ali free. Imagine looking at the size of life's battles without fear. What if you trust me and begin to believe that the barrier that blocked you from your destiny can be the platform God uses to propel you into your destiny? No longer will you be ruled by an imperfect past, difficult present, or grim future.

Think you'll have to be superwoman to do it? Spend thousands of dollars and dozens of years to get there? Learn eight languages to understand it? You're wrong!

I can show you one woman who faced many trials. Some because of the decisions she made and others because she was a victim of the choices of others. Still, she found a way to continue on her journey.

Survival can be a tricky road. It can be difficult to remember why we must press forward. Life can numb us so much we no longer want to remember who we are. If you're reading this book, it's because you want to remember. You want to try to survive again.

You want to believe that there is life after the memories . . . the pain . . . the rumors . . . and the lies. You want to get through today trusting that tomorrow will be better. You don't know how you'll keep going, only that you can't stop now. If these ring true, then you are on the same journey of survival that became the red carpet for Ruth's coming-out party.

Can you feel it? God is already beginning to restore you. With His help, please allow me to guide you through the story of Ruth so that you, too, can experience your collision with destiny.

1

Life Doesn't Always Go As Planned

Just because you make a change for the better doesn't mean you escape trouble. It only means your trouble has a promise.

In the days when the judges ruled, there was a famine in the land. So a man from Bethlehem in Judah, together with his wife and two sons, went to live for a while in the country of Moab. The man's name was Elimelek, his wife's name was Naomi, and the names of his two sons were Mahlon and Kilion. They were Ephrathites from Bethlehem, Judah. And they went to Moab and lived there.

Now Elimelek, Naomi's husband, died, and she was left with her two sons. They married Moabite women, one named Orpah and the other Ruth. After they had lived there about ten years, both Mahlon and Kilion also died, and Naomi was left without her two sons and her husband.

Ruth 1:1–5

We make idols out of so many things in our lives. Whether we're just getting by or finally getting ahead, we discover that cars, clothes, careers, relationships, and money all have a way of clouding our vision, pulling our focus away from God. Eventually, we learn that we cannot serve two masters. We must choose and prioritize what's most important to us. We have to draw the line between enjoying things and worshiping things.

In fact, it's usually not until we encounter trouble that we reassess what we consider valuable and learn that things are just that—things. Whether it's divorce, loss of income, death of a loved one, or some other life-changing moment, we finally find ourselves at a crossroads. What do we do when life doesn't go as planned? Will we become bitter? Or will we seek God in the midst of our loss and become better?

Ruth, a Moabite woman, grew up practicing the religion of her land. Although she was raised to worship many gods, there was only One who could prepare her for her destiny. When Ruth married Mahlon, she didn't marry just him. She married his God. Finding fulfillment in her marriage and her new faith, Ruth appeared to be living her dream.

We aren't told how much they enjoyed each other, but it seems clear from her grief that Ruth experienced an abiding love with her husband. She may have recognized her good fortune, or she might have taken it for granted. Regardless, she enjoyed ten years of living her dream—until her dream became her nightmare.

Ruth had to have felt like her world had shattered into thousands of irretrievable pieces. How could this have happened? This was not what she had expected! And it wasn't just her life that seemed to be crumbling to dust. Her father-in-law had already died, leaving behind his wife, Naomi, Ruth's beloved mother-in-law. Mahlon's brother also died. Now their family had no men to protect and provide for them. Ruth obviously had some hard choices before her.

What do you do when life doesn't go as planned? You've finally sown all the right seeds, yet all you reap in return is heartache. We hardly ever question God when things go as we want them to. But when we face trouble, we want answers. Where is God in the midst of our life's most painful disappointment?

Many times we feel so stunned by the blows we receive that we feel abandoned by God. How could He love us as His children yet allow these things to happen? Couldn't He have done something to prevent us from experiencing the bitter pain of our loss? Why would He allow this?

It's so easy to see Him when things are going our way. But are you willing to do the work it takes to discover Him in the midst of your disasters? He never promised there wouldn't be trials. He never promised we wouldn't have to wipe away some tears along the way.

What He has promised us is that we are not tested with any obstacle we can't overcome. And we will never have to face the harsh winds of life alone. God is there with us and has equipped us—long before He trusted us with the struggle. He knows better than we do what we can handle. He also knows what's required for us to mature into the masterpieces He designed.

My son is in the fifth grade, and I can already tell how his child-like tendencies are changing into full-blown adolescence. Before my very eyes my little boy is becoming a teen. I can tell in the way his thoughts are evolving and his mannerisms are changing.

I am usually the youngest mom at his class parties. To his peers this somehow makes me the coolest mom. It makes me the most afraid. I know too well the results of peer pressure. I can only imagine how my parents felt when they learned he was coming into the world—when I was barely a teen myself. On one side, their ministry was rising; on the other side, life was not going as planned.

Their courage during that time taught me a lesson I utilize now that I'm watching my son mature. You don't broadcast every fear. You don't give space to negativity when your life isn't going as planned. You have to be careful who you allow to speak into your life when you're most vulnerable. In your most difficult days you must remember to focus on the things that make you feel closest to God. When I was first pregnant with my son, I watched my parents go to church every Sunday to worship at His feet. Only a few people in the room knew in those early days, when the wound was yet fresh. My parents didn't have to expose their wound to people in order to give it to God. The beauty of prayer is that your heart is able to connect so purely with God. Our brokenness is most beautiful when we're in His presence. While Ruth was facing a tragic time in her life, she'd made a commitment to God over a decade prior.

When we decide to make Him ruler of our lives, we do so knowing that each day may not be easy, but each will serve a purpose. Just as Ruth could not anticipate that the death of her husband would be the beginning of her new life, we also lose sight of the fact that our troubles are only temporary. Even after having and losing it all, we must remember that whatever—or whomever—we lost, we have not lost God.

Sometimes He removes all the distractions from our lives so that we can focus solely on Him. Do not give up when life doesn't go as planned. Instead, remember that all things work together for our good when we live a Christ-led life (see Romans 8:28). The things that cause us the most pain are usually the roots that develop our true purpose. So weep, feel the pain, find a release for your anger, and sort through all the grief, but don't give up on God. He's there in the midst of it all.

As little girls, we dream about all the wonderful things we will do as adults. Often these include things like obtaining our education, falling in love, getting married, having children, and building a career. We imagine how perfect our lives will be when we grow up, our vision colored by our own innocence.

But soon enough we discover the many obstacles that life throws our way. Our education and career plans get put on hold. We fall in love but can't enjoy the level of trust we once hoped for in a husband. We struggle to conceive children or wrestle with the decision not to have them. We learn that parenting a baby doll is so much easier than the beautiful, high-maintenance real thing.

In short, we eventually learn we must recalibrate our expectations and turn our attention to who God made us to be, not the well-intentioned goals by which we used to define ourselves. We have to learn to rely on Him, which is bound to take us out of our comfort zone.

When you were younger, what was the plan you had for your life?

What has gotten in the way of this plan being realized?

How has the pain of losing your plan affected you?

How have your views on God changed as a result of the unexpected shift?

Prayer

God, I admit I'm lost, hurt, and confused. I've remained silent for too long, and now it's time to give my pain a voice. It's time for me to catch my breath and face what's ahead. I know I must accept that I'm broken before I can be healed. I need You, Lord. And like Ruth, I'm willing to follow You to my divine destiny. Amen.

2

Unmasking the Lone Ranger

*We often try to protect people from our trouble,
but if someone is willing to walk through it with
you, don't turn them away.*

Then [Naomi] arose with her daughters-in-law that she might return from the land of Moab, for she had heard in the land of Moab that the Lord had visited His people in giving them food. So she departed from the place where she was, and her two daughters-in-law with her; and they went on the way to return to the land of Judah. And Naomi said to her two daughters-in-law, "Go, return each of you to her mother's house. May the Lord deal kindly with you as you have dealt with the dead and with me. May the Lord grant that you may find rest, each in the house of her husband." Then she kissed them, and they lifted up their voices and wept. And they said to her, "No, but we will surely return with you to your people." But Naomi said, "Return, my daughters.

Why should you go with me? Have I yet sons in my womb, that they may be your husbands? Return, my daughters! Go, for I am too old to have a husband. If I said I have hope, if I should even have a husband tonight and also bear sons, would you therefore wait until they were grown? Would you therefore refrain from marrying? No, my daughters; for it is harder for me than for you, for the hand of the Lord has gone forth against me."

And they lifted up their voices and wept again; and Orpah kissed her mother-in-law, but Ruth clung to her.

Then she said, "Behold, your sister-in-law has gone back to her people and her gods; return after your sister-in-law."

Ruth 1:6–15 NASB

A good friend of mine went through a cancer scare. She called to let me know that she'd had some tests and the doctor wanted her to come in so they could discuss the results. I was due to go out of town on the day of her appointment, but I canceled my trip and told her I'd be there. She insisted that she would be fine going alone and found a thousand different ways to tell me canceling my trip was senseless. After several unsuccessful attempts to get me to change my mind, she finally gave in and allowed me to join her.

For me, being there wasn't something I did out of friendly obligation. I wanted to be there, because I needed her to remember that regardless of what the results were, she was not alone. I needed her to remember something we all need to hear when we're soaked by the storm.

Fear cannot isolate you if you allow love to surround you.

When your life has been shattered into pieces, it's hard to believe anyone would want to help you clean up the mess left behind. It's easier to push people away than to admit you're scared. It's easier to suffer in silence.

Sometimes it even feels easier to try to grieve by yourself. When you lose something or someone, it can be hard to imagine allowing anyone to grow close to you again—even someone who loves you and wants to comfort you. In the midst of your loss, you realize how alone you are, and you may fear that your heart will only ache more if you bare it to another soul. The irony is that isolation only compounds the pain.

Naomi had buried her husband and, ten years later, lost both of her sons. Realizing their wives, Orpah and Ruth, were still young women, Naomi encouraged them to go their separate ways. She realized that their only connection to her died when she buried her sons. Uncertain of what lay ahead of her, she pleaded with them to go back to their former lives.

We don't know her motivation for certain, but it seems clear that she cared about these young women and wanted them to find happiness for themselves rather than take a chance by following her back to Bethlehem. After all, they would be leaving Moab, the only place they had known as home. Not only would they have to start over, but they would be doing so in a strange, unfamiliar land. Even if Naomi was feeling sorry for herself, she clearly seemed to have her daughters-in-law's best interests at heart.

While Orpah heeded the older woman's counsel, Ruth refused to hear any of it. Naomi even told her that she should follow Orpah's example and return home. Yet Ruth refused just as stubbornly as her mother-in-law insisted. She was not going back. She was going forward—with Naomi.

How many times have we tried to protect people from going through trials with us? We pretend we're okay so others don't see just how broken we are. When we need people the most, we push them away, afraid they'll see our truth. Or worse . . . see our truth and then leave us.

Maybe this fear—of others seeing our broken hearts—keeps us from accepting what they have to offer. We can't bear the thought of being abandoned in the midst of what we're already experiencing. So instead of embracing the offer of assistance from others, we hold it together and act like we're strong enough to bear our burden alone. Besides, we don't want to be that person who's an emotional wreck, always needing someone else's support to limp along.

After all, it's hard to believe someone would volunteer to go through the trouble we can't bear to face ourselves. We don't want to drag them down to our level of sadness, disappointment, and frustration. We know we can't pretend that nothing is wrong, but we assume we can present a poker face without anyone calling our bluff. Sometimes we even want others to think we're stronger than we really are just so they'll leave us alone.

As difficult as it may be to trust again, you have to give people a chance to be there for you the way you've been there for them. When we are fragile, it's easier to be carried by love than to be left alone in our grief. Solitude is dangerous when grief is inescapable. Yes, you are capable of winning without the support of other people. With God's help, you have the endurance and the strength to make it, even if you don't have anyone on your team. But why do it alone if you don't have to?

Our Creator made us in His own image, to be social beings who need one another. He gave Eve to Adam so that he would not be alone in his endeavors. When they messed up and had to leave the garden of Eden, at least they still had each other. Yes, they had lost something precious and intimate with God, but He allowed them to stay together.

When Jesus came, thousands of years later, we see that even He needed people—His disciples. As He wrestled with the knowledge of His impending crucifixion, Christ took His disciples to another garden—this time Gethsemane. There He prayed and suffered, cried and sweat, knowing that He was about to be arrested and led to His death. While He could have endured His anguish alone, He chose to be with those He loved, who wanted to be there for Him—even if they couldn't stay awake.

This was not the only time He needed help. Bruised for our iniquities and wounded for our transgressions, He needed help to carry the cross God had given Him. It doesn't change the trajectory of your destiny or the power of your testimony when someone eases the burden of your cross. If anything, it lightens your load so that you can continue taking the next step, and then the next one, knowing that if you stumble, someone is there to lift you up and get you back on your feet.

Sometimes we know someone in one context—such as work or church—and feel reluctant to step outside of our role with them. We resist letting them see all the broken pieces of our lives from all the various areas of our lives. But occasionally we encounter someone who genuinely wants to go beyond the usual roles and polite small talk. If we keep them at arm's length or keep our mask in place, then we're not only missing out on what they have to offer; we're also denying them the opportunity to be blessed by serving someone—in this case you—in need.

When was the last time you made the decision to stand with someone instead of leaving in hard times?

Why did you make that decision?

How did this person respond? Were they grateful for your loyalty?

How do you acknowledge God in hard times? Do you view Him as your judge or lawyer? How does your view of Him translate to your relationships?

When was the last time someone was there for you when you needed a shoulder to cry on? Did you resist before letting them in? Or did you immediately accept the gift they offered?

Prayer

Lord, I know You will never leave me or forsake me. And I know that many times You use us, Your humble servants, as Your hands and feet. Please give me the wisdom to identify those people You've sent to me in every area of my life. Whether it's identifying someone who can help me navigate through my storm or being the one who sees them through theirs, show me how to trust someone with the pieces of my heart. Allow both of us to be blessed by the opportunity to share and bear one another's burdens. Amen.

3

Keep the Faith

When events in life get harder, that's when our faith must run deeper.

B ut Ruth replied, "Don't ask me to leave you and turn back. Wherever you go, I will go; wherever you live, I will live. Your people will be my people, and your God will be my God. Wherever you die, I will die, and there I will be buried. May the Lord punish me severely if I allow anything but death to separate us!" When Naomi saw that Ruth was determined to go with her, she said nothing more.

Ruth 1:16–18 NLT

Every New Year I start off with one resolution: lose weight. With renewed enthusiasm, I am dedicated to changing my eating habits, getting fit, and exercising consistently. This will be the year when fitness is truly a priority, when the desired results will occur so quickly that I'll be inspired to continue eating healthy food and taking care of my body. I'll fit into that pair of skinny jeans at the back of my closet and love the way I look more than ever.

But then, of course, as I make my preparations, I look ahead on the calendar. It should be easy, right? Since Thanksgiving turkey and Christmas goodies will be long gone, the day of the first month of the new year should be perfect for a new beginning. Then I remember I'll have to start on the second because we always have a big New Year's Day feast—you know, ham, black-eyed peas, and all the fixings.

But then I remember that I should wait to start till the fifth because my brother's birthday is on the fourth, and we usually have a special family dinner in his honor. Now that I think about it, it's more like a few weeks later. I like to host watch parties for all the big awards shows, and no one wants to eat celery and carrots. No matter how strong my good intentions are, somehow I always manage to find a hundred more reasons not to start my diet and exercise regimen. Before I know it, it's November, and I'm ten pounds heavier than I was when I made my resolution!

Last year was different, though. I went to the gym religiously. I learned which foods I could eat at our family feasts and remain healthy. The extra weight was literally falling off. Then a strange thing happened.

Around mid-February, I was no longer losing weight as rapidly. I'd drop a pound or two every few weeks, but not the number of pounds I'd become accustomed to. By March, I was discouraged. After working out with my trainer, I finally voiced my complaint. "How is it possible," I asked, "to work out harder but not lose any more weight?" The trainer smiled at me as if he'd heard this same complaint before. He explained that when you work out frequently, your body starts gaining muscle—so you continue to lose inches, but not necessarily weight. So even though I hadn't wavered in my commitment, and I knew changes were happening, I wasn't seeing the results in the way I expected.

Aha, I thought. So maybe I wasn't losing more pounds, but I was getting healthier. This incident made me realize that often we experience the same phenomenon in our spiritual lives. We get frustrated with God because we're doing all of the "right" things, but we aren't seeing any of the results we expect. It's even more difficult when you see the people around you prospering and you feel like God doesn't see your effort. We have to realize that just because God isn't showing up in the way we want, it doesn't mean He's not showing up. He can use anything to teach us; struggle just happens to get our attention the quickest. Our dilemmas are but a speck on His masterpiece; trust that things are working out for your good.

As Ruth looked into the eyes of her mother-in-law, surely she thought about the commitment she had made to her husband— and her husband's God. Although it appeared that life wasn't working in her favor, something inside of her refused to go back to the way things had been. Naomi begged Ruth to turn around and go back where she came from. But Ruth refused to give up.

From her limited perspective, it didn't look like her new faith was working. Her dedication didn't appear to be paying off. Little did she know that God, in His infinite wisdom, was working it out in ways she couldn't even imagine, let alone see yet. All she knew was that she couldn't give up on her new faith. She couldn't just abandon her mother-in-law and pretend that she didn't care.

Ruth was losing inches, but carrying the same weight.

Don't let discouragement block your blessing. Just because it doesn't look like God is working for you doesn't mean your commitment isn't paying off. You don't know when or where you'll reap your harvest, but you can trust that God sees your seeds. Even if you don't see it now, you're moving toward your destiny.

Like a dieter struggling to persevere, we want visible results and we want them fast. When we experience a painful loss in our lives, we long for things to return to normal. Perhaps we can't imagine our circumstances ever improving, but we can at least hope that God will comfort us, provide for us, and protect us during the storm swirling in our midst. When the storm doesn't stop immediately, however, we often assume that God either hasn't heard our prayers or doesn't care.

But neither is true. My body grew stronger and healthier even though I no longer saw the pounds melting away. In the same way, our faith, which may have grown flabby from disuse, grows stronger when we trust that God hears our cries and knows our needs. We can rest in the knowledge that He's making us stronger no matter how helpless we may feel.

Journal

I've been frustrated with God. I know it's not popular to admit that, and we're supposed to always vocalize our faith. I've felt invisible to Him, and it made me bitter. You don't become bitter over night; it's a defense mechanism you gradually create in order to never be hurt again. I began to constantly relive memories of hurt. I called it protection; the world called it bitter. Eventually I realized I couldn't let that consume me. When I didn't understand why things weren't working the way I wanted, I needed to think ahead and focus on hope. We must continue to stay in His will even when we feel we're out of His vision.

Have you ever started a diet or self-improvement program? What were the results? How did you remain motivated during the process?

What are you hoping God will change for the better in your life?

What have you remained committed to even though the results haven't been evident? Why?

What has made you give up in the past? What will make you stay faithful now?

Prayer

Lord, please help me to remember that it takes time to grow and change. Remind me that there is time between when a seed is planted and when the fruit is produced. Give me patience and stamina. Help me not to grow weary and become shortsighted. Grant me Your strength so that I may persevere through the process, knowing that even when I can't see the results I want, You're still there for me. Amen.

4

Don't Let Life Change Your Name

"It ain't what they call you, it's what you answer to."

—attributed to W. C. Fields

So the two women went on until they came to Bethlehem. When they arrived in Bethlehem, the whole town was stirred because of them, and the women exclaimed, "Can this be Naomi?"

"Don't call me Naomi," she told them. "Call me Mara, because the Almighty has made my life very bitter."

Ruth 1:19–20

remember it like it was yesterday. I was just months from celebrating my third wedding anniversary, and a month after that another woman would be having my husband's child. I wasn't ready to quit my marriage, though. I didn't want to let her have him. So I stayed and covered my pain with arrogance. I hurled as many insults at her as I could. I made her our enemy because it was easier than seeing her as his lover. I avoided the truth until I finally admitted I was falling in love with being bitter. It felt good to make someone else feel the pain I had been dealt. I foolishly thought that my targets were my only victims. I never realized I was the biggest loser. I allowed my inability to accept a truth I couldn't change to eat away at my heart.

I remember well talking to my marriage counselor after a particularly hard day. She was encouraging me to put forth my best effort if I was committed to making my marriage work. I nodded my head while she talked through my cell phone. When I felt the water begin to form in my eyes, I hurried to end the call as quickly as I could. As I closed my eyes and finally let the tears stream down my face, I remember thinking, *I want to be bitter.* I didn't stumble into bitterness. I made a decision to make one person suffer. I just wish I had realized that bitterness cannot be contained. Once you let it in, it affects everything around you.

Still, like Naomi, I wanted to be bitter. Maybe I didn't want to change my name like she did, but my feeling seemed just as intense.

Changing her name, though—now that's bitter. The first thing we learn about a person is his or her name. It is the way we introduce ourselves to the world. When we agree to terms on something, such as a contract or a loan, we sign our name. Our name is how we want to be remembered. Our name represents who we are and who we are called to be.

Right from the beginning in Genesis, it's clear God considers our names important, too. Adam's name signified his role as the first man, while Eve's name reflected her relationship to Adam. God charged both of them with naming all the plants, animals, and living creatures in the garden of Eden. Yes, our names matter—to us, to other people, and to God.

After burying her husband and two sons in a foreign land, Naomi was bitter. So bitter that she decided to change her name to Mara, another way of saying the same thing. She mourned through an endless night and couldn't imagine ever feeling joy again. She didn't feel like the person she used to be, so she figured she might as well become what she felt. Her grief had consumed all that was inside her, right down to the essence of her identity.

Naomi lost touch with her own unique personality and purpose. When we experience a crisis, we become disoriented, confused, and uncertain about what's what. The world we once knew has forever changed—our expectations, our goals, our journeys. Drained of strength, certainty, and significance, we no longer remember who we are or even how we arrived at such a place in our lives.

Suffering from a case of spiritual amnesia, we allow our losses and mistakes to redefine us. *Liar, cheater, dummy, fool, adulterer*—life gives us countless titles if we let it. Some may even reflect mistakes we've made or trials we're still enduring. At some point, whether deliberately or inadvertently, we've all done or experienced something we're not proud of—and some decisions even led to devastation. Without a strong foundation to ground us, in the midst of our pain we may face an identity crisis. Will we remember who we've always been, or will this hurt be what now defines us?

When the memories of what should have been invade your soul and shake your core, whatever you do, don't let it change your name. You know how perfume can subtly linger where the wearer has been? Many women become so known by the scent they wear that it's easy to identify the trail of their presence. You don't want the agony of your pain to be the aroma that lingers behind when you exit a room. You don't want to reward misery by allowing it to be the center of your life. Instead of the pleasant association of your true self, you only compound the smell of fear when you make it your trademark.

Don't reward misery by allowing it to be the center of your life. Don't give the person who has injured you any more time in the spotlight. Don't allow your life's headlines to keep repeating old news. We have to be careful about the feelings we allow on the center stage of our hearts. For "out of the abundance of the heart the mouth speaks" (Matthew 12:34 NKJV). When we focus only on what we've lost, who has hurt us, and why we're afraid, we only inflate the power of these emotions and events over us. When our anger, pain, and fear eclipse our identities, we tend to lose sight of what's true about ourselves and about God.

In our pain, how then do we reconcile our true feelings with our faith? Sure, we know what we're supposed to say and think. We know that vengeance belongs to the Lord and that others will reap what they sow. We know the "right answers" and how we *should* be feeling. When you've cried for months and months, though, it gets difficult to believe that weeping will only endure for a night. When the numbness persists and you can't even feel your heart anymore, it's hard to break the spell.

But you can get through this if you stay true to the person God created you to be. Even when you feel labeled by life's losses, you must never let the pain push you into being someone you're not—someone hopeless, angry, bitter, resentful. It doesn't mean you can't feel those moments. We all have times when we're overwhelmed with emotion, but we have to find a way out.

Who have you been and who do you want to be? What has your name meant to you over the course of your life so far? Decide what you want your name, your legacy, to be and declare it over your life. Do you want to be remembered as hostile, vicious, or spiteful? Or do you want the world to remember how you survived and learned to live again?

Naomi was stricken with grief. She wanted to face the pain alone, but God allowed Ruth to be a part of her journey. Ruth, someone who knew her in better days, could remind Naomi who she once was. Don't miss the moments when God sends you a reminder of who you were meant to be. Joy can only come in the morning if you remember to open the curtains and let in the morning light.

Journal

Painful circumstances and other people will often try to give us a new name. Reinforced by social media and old-fashioned gossip, our new names are often repeated enough until we accept them as our own. If our circumstances are unbearable, with no relief in sight, then we may forget who we really are. We hear other people talking and begin to answer to new names like Bitter, Ashamed, and Victim. We must remain firmly grounded in our identity as God's precious child, not how we feel in the midst of devastation or how other people describe us.

> How do you define yourself? What words would you use to describe who you really are?

> How do you want to be remembered?

When have you allowed your pain to make you forget your destiny?

How would the healed you be different from the hurt you?

God, help me to see myself the way You see me. Open my eyes so that I can see beyond this broken place. I want to discover my potential. I want to believe there is life after this. Remind me of the truth of Your Word, "that all things work together for good to those who love God, to those who are the called according to His purpose" (Romans 8:28 NKJV). When I feel I've lost my purpose, help me to remember that You have one greater in store for me. Amen.

5

Stick With What You Know

When life leaves you empty, you must return to the
foundation of what you know for sure.

I went out full, and the Lord has brought me home again
   empty. Why do you call me Naomi, since the Lord has
testified against me, and the Almighty has afflicted me?"
   So Naomi returned, and Ruth the Moabitess her daughter-
in-law with her, who returned from the country of Moab. Now
they came to Bethlehem at the beginning of barley harvest.

Ruth 1:21–22 NKJV

Last Christmas, my daughter wanted a Dora the Explorer bicycle. After driving across town, checking several stores, waiting in line, and finally getting the bicycle, I was elated. I couldn't wait to see her face when she saw the bike for the first time. On Christmas Eve, after wrapping the last of the kids' gifts and placing them under the tree, I remembered the bike.

Tired and eager to relax, I quickly started putting it together. Once I opened the box and saw the pieces, I didn't bother with the instructions. The pieces just looked like they would fit. After all, it was a Dora bike; how hard could it be?

As it turned out, it was *much* harder than it looked. After several attempts, I took everything apart again, read the instructions, and finally discovered the way things were supposed to go all along. I laughed at myself and realized that so often this is the way things go in life. We jump in and think we know how all the pieces fit, only to learn the hard way that our way is not the right way. We have to go back to the certainty of our instructions.

So much of this process has to do with letting go of former expectations and embracing the new, undeniable reality. Like many parents, I couldn't imagine how putting a kid's bike together could be that complicated. But then I encountered dozens of little pieces, many resembling each other, and realized that my expectations were way off base. I gained a newfound respect for all the bikes, scooters, and other toys my parents had assembled for me!

Sometimes in life, we expect a relationship, an event, or a transaction to go smoothly—and then discover that the reality is much different. Conversations and interactions become more complex, nuanced by personal agendas and hidden motives. Maybe we missed the obvious signs because of our own unwillingness to see the truth. Or maybe we were overconfident in our ability to adjust to change. Regardless of the catalyst, life continually presents us with moments that force us to revise our expectations and recalculate our present path.

Ten years before her crisis, Naomi found herself looking at all the pieces of her life and thinking she knew exactly how things would turn out. She did everything she knew to do, everything that made perfect sense. But in the wake of such devastating loss, life began whispering, letting her know that God's plan was better than her own.

No matter what seems probable or likely to happen, the reality is that we never see all the variables involved in the equation. Only God has a perspective that is constant, never changing, and big enough to encompass all the ups and downs of our journey. We can't see what's around the bend or over the next hill, but He can. Often we're humbled and forced to confront our limitations when our expectations go unfulfilled. We can second-guess and plan all we want, but ultimately we cannot control everything that happens in our lives.

We have all had these moments, these devastating blows that leave us lost. In our confusion, we seek something to numb our pain. We seek distractions to keep us from remembering the disappointment of our plans falling apart. Instead of getting frustrated and throwing the scattered pieces of my daughter's bike in the trash—which I was momentarily tempted to do—I had to take a deep breath and start over. It wasn't easy, I was tired, and I felt foolish for not reading the instructions in the first place. But the only way to fulfill my little girl's dream the next morning was to start over and begin again.

Naomi had to return, humbled and grief-stricken, back to the place where she had started. It couldn't have been easy or her first choice. When she and her family left Bethlehem, they did so with a spirit of adventure in the face of necessity. She had her husband's strength to rely on as well as the joy of mothering her sons. Going back would only mean confronting the absence of her husband and sons once again. Going home would not offer any real solace and, in fact, might only make matters worse. But still, where else could she turn?

Sometimes the only way to move forward is to go back to what we know and start again. Naomi didn't just go home so that she could start over. After losing her children and husband, she had also lost the significant roles in which many women find their purpose and identity. Now more than ever, she needed to return to the people who could help her remember who she really was.

How many times have we had to start over? New career. Foreclosed home. Divorce. School. Life has a way of giving us the option of humbling ourselves or numbing ourselves. Do we try to move on as if nothing has happened, or do we dare admit that we must start again? Often our pride prevents us from admitting that life has dealt us a blow. We pretend that we have it all together. We invent stories that suggest we aren't as broken as we actually are.

But it's okay for things not to be okay. When life makes us start over, we must do it in a safe place. Never be so prideful that you miss a chance to be vulnerable with those who know you. There's something special about being able to show someone your scars.

Naomi's return home reminds us that we all must return to the source of our strength. And when you're seeking refuge, never forget the safest place there is—in the Master's arms.

Journal

When I was growing up, I used to joke with my father that I was never moving out of my parents' home. I told them I'd be at least forty before I ever purchased a box. When I decided to show them I could make it on my own and finally moved out, I promised myself I'd never ever move back in.

If only I had known what I was promising! It took being thousands of miles away from home for me to realize how much you can lose yourself trying to find yourself. I thought because my heart was in the right place things would work out. I didn't realize we can do all the right things, but if it's with the wrong person or at the wrong time, we won't get the desired results. There's a process we must endure to get the promise. Anytime the promise is no longer clear, we must reassess where we are in the process. Did we skip a step? Toss the instructions and go for what we know? Regardless of how off track we think we are, we can always ask God to reorder our steps.

What is the last time you remember being happy, safe, or free?

What was it about that period that contributed to your joy?

What's one thing from your childhood that still makes your heart smile? Can you return to it for some comfort in the midst of your present pain?

Who are the people you can count on to remind you who you really are?

Prayer

Lord, somewhere along the way I got lost. I don't know how I got here or how I can make things better. I just know that I don't want to live like this anymore. God, help me to build my life with You as the foundation. I know that time and relationships will always add to my burden, but when it all gets to be too much, I hope You'll help me see where I went wrong. Even if that means starting all over. Amen.

6

Do What You Can

It's so easy to let rejection stop us from trying, but you must be dedicated to survive.

Now there was a wealthy and influential man in Bethlehem named Boaz, who was a relative of Naomi's husband, Elimelech.

One day Ruth the Moabite said to Naomi, "Let me go out into the harvest fields to pick up the stalks of grain left behind by anyone who is kind enough to let me do it."

Naomi replied, "All right, my daughter, go ahead." So Ruth went out to gather grain behind the harvesters. And as it happened, she found herself working in a field that belonged to Boaz, the relative of her father-in-law, Elimelech.

Ruth 2:1–3 NLT

never thought the role of author would be added to my list of accomplishments. I didn't think that writing could be a gift. Everyone does it, right? As a matter of fact, it wasn't until I started blogging as a way to release my own pain that I realized not everyone has the words their hearts are trying to speak. It is because of that blog that this book is even in your hands. So when I learned that I had something in common with another writer, Joanne, I had to share her story with you.

Joanne had her first child at twenty-eight. After an impressive collegiate career, including a year's study in Paris, she and her husband started a family. Nearly five months after the birth of her daughter, however, Joanne and her husband divorced. She had done everything "right," but her presumably perfect life hit rock bottom. She didn't have a job and was forced to live on government assistance. Things weren't going as expected—not at all.

Nevertheless, Joanne had to keep going and began by thinking about who she was and what she loved to do. Long before this detour on her journey, Joanne had loved writing short stories. Maybe she couldn't fix her marriage, maybe her future was uncertain, but she knew one thing for sure: She could still write. She knew she had some talent and appreciated the way her writing became a wonderful distraction. Soon her stories grew into a full-length book. Rejected by twelve publishers before reaching millions of readers around the world, Joanne, better known as J. K. Rowling, is the mastermind behind Harry Potter. She became richer than the Queen of England—literally. Rowling's success, though, remains rooted in the seeds of her struggle. It didn't come easily or all at once. She just kept writing and doing what she knew to do.

We cannot allow rejection to convince us to stop trying. Whether it be in the pursuit of our heart's desires or the belief in our dreams, our dedication is what separates us from others. Ruth was not allowed to glean in the fields with the other women, but she didn't let the rejection stop her from doing what she could. It may have been the leftovers, but something was better than nothing. Sometimes what appears to be left over can become the seeds for future harvests. If you're committed to a new life, you have to be willing to keep going without seeing an immediate return.

J. K. Rowling had no way of knowing that her books would break publishing records for selling millions of copies around the world. She probably could not have imagined the successful film franchise that resulted from her amazing imagination. But she knew she loved to write and that she could tell a good story. She knew those things to be true about her no matter what else had happened. So even as an impoverished single mom, she did what she could.

Or think of it this way. Most mothers will tell you that the most exciting part of pregnancy is when they finally see their stomach swell with the new life inside. Before there are any outward signs of growth, their body has been making all these internal changes. Staying awake past seven feels like punishment. The smell of tacos makes them sick. And almost everyone seems to have a personal mission to get on their nerves in some way. . . . Well, okay, maybe that was just me. None of it matters, though, when your body starts welcoming the new life inside you. Suddenly, others can see that you aren't just being lazy, picky, or irritable. You are birthing something.

When circumstances restrict you from being able to do certain things, don't treat it as punishment. Just know that it's a part of your growing process. The common denominator between a pregnant woman whose body is no longer the same and a particular single mother whose "perfect life" fell apart is dedication to a new life.

When you face limitations, focus on what you still have and what you still can accomplish. It may not seem like much, but you never know how your seeds planted today might blossom tomorrow. So much of restoration is simply about getting through each day, even if that simply means showering, getting dressed, cooking, cleaning, running errands, or whatever needs doing. In the midst of the mundane, you can still discover a new path or an innovative idea. Limitations only limit you if you let them. Instead, let them make you more creative, resourceful, and determined in pursuit of your dreams.

Choose to believe that, in spite of your rejection or restrictions, there is hope for you yet. Ruth couldn't glean with the rest of the women. She already decided she couldn't go back to her homeland. She had made a promise to her mother-in-law that she intended to keep. As a widowed woman in a foreign culture, her options were more than limited—they were almost nonexistent. But Ruth made the best of her situation and did what she could. Don't be discouraged; what you see as restrictions could really just be preparation and protection.

Journal

It's not easy to keep your hope fresh when your pain is rotting you away. I remember so vividly asking God why my marriage wasn't working when I was trying to do everything the right way. Dinner was ready, the children were bathed, and the house was clean. I was trying to be a Proverbs 31 woman every day, and I couldn't understand why things were falling apart. You can do all the right things, but you can't do them for the wrong reasons. I wanted to be a "perfect" wife to prove that I was worthy of love, not because our love inspired me. I asked my husband to define me, but I didn't like the definition I received. It hurt each time his actions confirmed my insecurities. I needed that pain, though; without that pain this moment would not exist. Had I never experienced heartbreak, I never would have discovered why joy is worth fighting for.

One of the most difficult times in my short marriage was dealing with an unexpected pregnancy. Three years in, I learned my husband and another woman were expecting a child together. I had seen all the signs, and after months of arguing and denials, finally I had proof that I wasn't going crazy. I was more relieved than hurt. That's not to say I wasn't hurt at all. The pregnancy was just confirmation of my suspicion. I remember trying to support my husband during that time by buying baby clothes and sending money to help with the pregnancy expenses. I'd been humiliated, and now I was helping to clean up their mess. I asked my marriage counselor repeatedly why I had to be the bigger person when they'd done all the wrong. I wanted permission to be bitter, but she wouldn't give it. Each time I felt bitterness creep into my heart, I bought something else for the baby with tears in my eyes.

Eventually, to everyone's surprise—including my husband's—a paternity test showed he was not this baby's father. Although I was relieved, the damage had been done. The affair had already been confirmed.

And I needed that pain. I needed that disappointment. It forced me to find a release on a blog I thought no one would ever see. No one knows what purpose can form from your pain, but if you let the hurt blind you, you'll never see that some collisions are necessary for our destiny.

What was your first encounter with a major personal rejection?

What did you learn from it?

Did you give up after you were rejected? Why or why not?

What's keeping you from trying once again to pursue your destiny?

Prayer

God, help me to see that rejection is simply Your divine direction. Thank You for closing the doors that weren't part of Your plan. I'm grateful that You opened a window and made a way of escape when I had chosen my will over Your own. I ask that You cover me as I guard my heart from the infection of disappointment. I trust that I'm not in this alone. Amen.

7

You Never Know Who's Watching

"Live your life in such a way that if someone lied about you, no one would believe it."

—based on 1 Peter 2:12

Just then Boaz arrived from Bethlehem and greeted the harvesters, "The Lord be with you!"

"The Lord bless you!" they answered.

Boaz asked the overseer of his harvesters, "Who does that young woman belong to?"

Ruth 2:4-5

It was three in the morning and I had just achieved optimum REM sleep when I heard a knock on my bedroom door. Like most parents, I could tell by the knock which child it was: Makenzie. I opened the door expecting to hear her express fear and then jump in my bed. Instead I heard, "Can I ride my bicycle?"

It took some time before the request registered in my brain. How long had she been awake? What was she doing up? Where was my pillow? Now fully awake, I moved closer to the light so that she could see my face, specifically my eyes. Immediately she ran back upstairs to her room. I'd mastered my mother's age-old technique of giving "the look." It had taken some time, but now it was working like a charm. No longer would I have to remind my children to return to their best behavior with a quick chat in the bathroom; one look and they knew. The look continues to come in handy. If something is broken or I suspect a story has a few holes, I give the look and instantly they spill the beans.

There are times, though, when I don't need a look or the words to get the truth. Sometimes they tell on themselves—with sticky fingers from candy or a stain from a marker on their clothes after someone was inspired to write on a wall. You don't have to be a detective to get to the bottom of some dilemmas.

How many times have you watched the news as the camera pans to a person in an orange jumpsuit—their eyes bugged out, movements erratic, and voice shaky—and instantly you assume they're as guilty as they look? Or think about how some of our most sensational television shows revolve around criminal cases. Immediately, the audience determines whether the suspect is innocent or guilty based on how the alleged criminal looks. Sometimes right, sometimes wrong, the viewer plays a guessing game based largely on how a suspect reacts under pressure.

Now more than ever, we all know how important appearances can be. And it's not just our fashion sensibility, either. Body language, tone of voice, and emotional intelligence all factor in to the way other people perceive us. Studies have shown how people often come to resemble the person others see them to be. For instance, students in an elementary school class who were told they were in the "gifted" group performed better than before. Similarly, when students were told that they were "remedial," they demonstrated more behavior problems and performed lower academically.

No wonder, then, that we must be true to ourselves, especially when forming the perceptions from which others will attempt to label us. How you respond often reveals whether there is any validity in the accusations waged against you. You cannot control who judges you, but you can be responsible for portraying the most authentic version of yourself. It doesn't stop the judgment, but it allows others to see your truth whether they like it or not. When you remain true to your values and carry yourself with dignity, then others can talk all they want. Your truth will trump their misperceptions.

Ruth stood out not just by being a foreigner but also because of how confidently she conducted herself—despite how she may have felt inside. She did not pretend to be something or someone she wasn't. Anyone could tell that she was not an Israelite, that she didn't look like the other women in the village. But she didn't try to conform and lose her ties to her homeland. She knew who she was and could live out of this confidence.

No wonder others did a double take. Even if she had been from Bethlehem, she would have stood out for her poise and the natural beauty of her composure. As Boaz stared from his favorite spot in the field, overlooking the rewards of his entrepreneurial endeavors, his eyes stopped on the stranger straggling behind the other gleaners. Who was this woman? What compelled her to trail behind and sort through the leftover grain for sustenance? She was different, all right. From where he stood, she just appeared to be a loner, a woman who didn't belong with the crowd.

Ruth didn't know she was being watched. As lonely and fearful as she may have been, her isolation became her platform. Ruth was more noticeable on her own than she ever would've been in the crowd. There's something to be said about not fitting in.

From the inside looking out, we wonder what's wrong with us. We feel self-conscious and wonder why others aren't willing to accept us for who we are. We think, *Is it my hair? Is it my weight? Am I not smart enough? What is it about me that keeps me from being good enough for them?*

Sometimes we even go to great measures to hide our real beauty so that we can blend in with those around us. Whether it's dressing like everyone else when we long to express our unique style or changing the way we speak in order to tell people what they want to hear, we disguise our true dignity.

Then we come to view our separation as punishment, wondering what we did that landed us here and how we can fit in. From the inside we let our differences torment us until we no longer desire to belong. We accept that this may always be our fate and things will not get better. We allow struggle to rob us of our hope.

You never know what giving up on yourself teaches others about you. Be careful, especially in trials, to govern your actions with grace and hope. Your ability to maintain class in the midst of a storm is an indication of what you believe about yourself. You may feel shaken and unsure, but you mustn't let your uniqueness prevent you from moving forward with grace.

It bears repeating: You cannot control who judges you, but you can be responsible for portraying the most authentic version of yourself. It doesn't stop the judgment, but it allows others to see your truth whether they like it or not. It's hard for gossip and rumors to continue when everyone can see the truth for themselves.

There's an old saying, "Never let them see you sweat." Notice it doesn't say, "Do not sweat at all." It just says you don't need to let the world see when the pressure is getting to you. Learn to vent in a safe place so that you can pull it together when it counts. In the safety of her home with Naomi, Ruth could acknowledge her fears. But when it was time to face the day, she greeted others with the strength poured into her at home.

Ruth's graceful tenacity made Boaz sit up and take notice. She wasn't like everyone else. She was her own woman.

Be careful how you handle this storm; you never know who's watching.

Journal

When I was young and adjusting to motherhood as a teenager, my heroes were women like Cathy Hughes and Oprah—women who had faced struggles similar to my own and persevered to succeed. They refused to accept the labels others tried to stick on them. As they grew and matured, they became more comfortable with their talents, gifts, and abilities and refused to let other people write the script for them.

Women like these resemble Ruth in their courage, strength, and resilience. They remind us of what it means to beat the odds and still be yourself. They make it clear that you don't have to sell out to be successful—in fact, you'll go further if you just be yourself. These women continue to inspire me to take risks and never look back. I think Ruth would be proud!

Who is someone you currently admire? Why? What is it about them that has earned your respect?

How has their journey affected your own?

What would someone learn about you if they saw you in your weakest moment?

If you are the only reflection of Christ that people see, would He be pleased with how you represent Him?

As I strive to be more like You, I hope that You will help me to remember my life is not my own. In anger, disappointment, and frustration, I want to be able to represent Your sacrifice on Calvary. Help me to look beyond myself and seek the grace that will make You proud of how I handled my test. Amen.

8

Your Enemy Becomes Your Footstool

Other people's gossip about you can often become the best advertisement for your authenticity.

The foreman replied, "She is the young woman from Moab who came back with Naomi. She asked me this morning if she could gather grain behind the harvesters. She has been hard at work ever since, except for a few minutes' rest in the shelter."

Boaz went over and said to Ruth, "Listen, my daughter. Stay right here with us when you gather grain; don't go to any other fields. Stay right behind the young women working in my field. See which part of the field they are harvesting, and then follow them. I have warned the young men not to treat you roughly. And when you are thirsty, help yourself to the water they have drawn from the well."

Ruth 2:6–9 NLT

Years ago I heard a song in a movie trailer, and the lyrics, combined with the soulful rendering, made me want to be a better writer. Weird, I know. There was just something about this singer creating a sound that had never been heard before that made me want to create something special, too. My little secret, my creative muse, soon went from being music's best-kept secret to becoming the incomparable Adele.

Beloved for her talent and commitment to being her authentic self, she inspired me to remember that talent and authenticity can live in the same place. Adele was discovered after posting a few songs on MySpace. The news of her great talent spread until she could no longer go unnoticed. She could not be ignored. She didn't need all the hype of a marketing team and tabloid gossip to become a household name. People could feel who she really is just by listening to her music.

In case you're not familiar with her, Adele is not your typical pop music star. She's full-figured and proud of it, unwilling to starve herself into someone else's body image. She's not blonde or known for revealing skin at awards shows. She doesn't seem concerned with what others tweet about her. The girl is about the music! Her success provides another great reminder that quality and talent will always rise to the top. When you pursue your passions and dedicate yourself to bringing your dreams alive, then what you do speaks louder than what any social media buzz can generate.

If we're true to ourselves, then we don't have to worry about what others may say about us. Our actions and authenticity will speak louder than anyone else's words. We have to realize that some people will always be tempted to misconstrue our actions and spread lies about us. They thrive on tearing others down so that they can feel better about themselves. These people are never satisfied because they're always comparing and looking to external sources for approval instead of fulfilling the destiny for which they were designed.

Ruth learned quickly that her arrival into a strange land acquired the attention of many. As a new convert, she may have faced some speculation on the validity of her faith. Perhaps they even questioned her motives. Why would a young woman stay with this aging, grief-stricken woman? What would motivate her to wander out in the fields, looking for leftover grain in someone else's fields? Surely she must be up to something. What was her game?

The rumors spread so rapidly that everyone knew her story before getting to know her. The conversations about her, whether idle chatter or malicious gossip, made her journey more difficult. It's one thing to struggle; it's another to struggle on stage. When private battles become public performances, it's hard to remain true to yourself. Who doesn't feel self-conscious when they know everyone is watching and scrutinizing every move they make?

Yet how could she have ever guessed that the town's gossiping about her would lead to her being blessed? Without even realizing it, they were giving information to the man who would change her life. Instead of judging her based on idle rumors, Boaz witnessed Ruth's determination firsthand. He saw for himself the kind of person she was. He didn't have to rely on hearsay and secondhand reports because he had watched her himself.

People who support and care about you will seek out the truth. They won't assume that everything they hear about you is true. If they have integrity and are committed to living authentically, they will reserve judgment until they have firsthand evidence. Quality attracts quality just as iron sharpens iron. Boaz was a good man and recognized the goodness in Ruth. The speculation and assumptions of other people meant nothing to him.

Right before her eyes, Ruth's enemies became her footstool. Don't let the possibility of your name being tarnished keep you from doing right. If you're so busy defending yourself from idle rumors and salacious gossip, you won't have the energy to stay on your journey. If you dedicate all of your concentration to the whispers of others, how will you hear when He comes calling for you?

My biggest concern when I had my son at fourteen was what other people would think about me. I knew that news would spread relatively quickly, so I needed to brace myself for what I thought I'd hear. I called myself every name in the book thinking that it would somehow make it hurt less once the rumor mill started. Instead of strengthening myself with messages of hope, I fed myself with the negativity I thought was coming.

When the gossip finally reached my ears, it was just confirmation of what I already thought. I had no hope to combat my insecurities, because I fed myself a steady diet of self-hate. I lowered my self-esteem to prepare for the thoughts that would come about my past. Maybe if it was low enough the hate would miss my heart and hurt less. It took more pain for me to realize that God wasn't asking me to lower myself. I needed to look up to Him.

How has your life been affected by gossip?

How has it deterred you from excelling in a particular area? How has it motivated you to pursue your goals?

Ruth found the strength to live in the face of gossip. How can you withstand your critics and find the strength to tell your own story?

If people are able to only see you and hear your story from others, what do you hope the combination says about you?

God, help me to remember that if I don't learn to live again, rumors will define me. I know You've placed too much inside of me for gossip to stop me. I trust You to take even my most shameful moment and use it to help me reach my destiny. I just pray You give me the grace to hold my head high when the whispers begin to weigh me down. Amen.

9

He Knew You
Before He Blessed You

Don't let rumors shame you into believing God can't use you.

At this, she bowed down with her face to the ground. She asked him, "Why have I found such favor in your eyes that you notice me—a foreigner?"

Boaz replied, "I've been told all about what you have done for your mother-in-law since the death of your husband—how you left your father and mother and your homeland and came to live with a people you did not know before. May the Lord repay you for what you have done. May you be richly rewarded by the Lord, the God of Israel, under whose wings you have come to take refuge."

Ruth 2:10–12

What happens when you insist on preparing for pain by hurting yourself? You forget what it's like to feel anything else. Either they're beating you up or you're beating yourself up. So who is protecting your hope when you're nursing your shame?

I didn't believe I deserved the same type of love a virgin should receive. I couldn't have a beautiful picture because I'd already done too much damage. The most I could hope for was to attempt for a close facsimile.

Sure, I thought, *I may have to share my husband, but that is the cost for sharing myself so early.* We loved each other—at least we said we did—but I think what really drew us together was the idea that we represented wholeness for one another. We were both too broken to truly love each other, but we did love the picture we created after the past we had messed up.

I didn't trust that grace was sufficient for me.

Newly released convicts often forget what it's like to be free. Confined for so long, they don't remember how to function independently. They continue to think of themselves as nothing more than the verdict for their crimes. They assume others see them this way, and they themselves may not know how to define themselves apart from their past mistakes. And, unfortunately, many of them end up making the same mistakes again, only to return to confinement.

We may not be incarcerated, but we all experience this dilemma. And you know why our history repeats itself? Because instead of letting the past teach us, we allow it to define us. Like prisoners newly released from confinement, we have to decide how we will process our past mistakes and misjudgments. If we don't deliberately choose to learn from what we've been through, we often set ourselves up to go through something like it again. If we don't learn from our mistakes and allow God to use them in order to change us, then we get stuck on a treadmill of repetition.

Either our obstacles in life hover over us forever or we find a way to climb on top of them and advance to the next level of our destiny. They either crush us from the burden of their weight or become the stepping-stone, the launching pad, of our greatness.

When people recognize us but don't exactly remember how they know us, we use shared memories to jog their recollection. Oddly enough, though, when God does exceedingly, abundantly above all that we may ask or think, we begin to doubt whether He remembers who we really are. *I don't think You meant to give this to me*, we think. *I'm the one who wrote bad checks. I'm the one who got an abortion. I'm the one who got the DUI. I'm the one who told those lies. I'm the one who has that terrible secret.* We find all of these excuses for why we don't deserve to be blessed.

How long will you allow your past to shackle you?

When Ruth asked Boaz, "Why have I found such favor in your eyes that you notice me—a foreigner?" she gives us a peek into her mindset. She had been keeping the faith, doing the right things, and becoming a stronger person, but a part of her still didn't believe she was worthy of being blessed. She assumed Boaz saw her as nothing more than a stranger, a woman from Moab who had wandered into Bethlehem. She received a tremendous opportunity, seemingly out of nowhere, and still didn't recognize it as her harvest.

In order to receive the blessings of God, we must quiet that voice inside of us that wonders, *Why me?* Ruth wanted to know why Boaz would bless a stranger; little did she know, he knew exactly who she was. He had been watching her from afar and respected her hard work ethic and dedicated commitment to her mother-in-law. He appreciated Ruth's willingness to move out of her comfort zone and venture into a foreign land. No matter what other people might have been saying about her, Boaz knew the truth.

When God uses someone to sow into your life, don't discredit it because you think they don't know you. They obviously know enough to give you an opportunity for advancement. They clearly see something in you, something true and authentic, that they want to invest in. Other people don't have to know every mistake and misdemeanor from your past in order to appreciate who you are becoming.

Better yet, God knows you and that's enough. He knows your struggle and still sees your worth. He knew you before He blessed you. Nothing you've done or will do can surprise your Father in heaven. No matter how badly you mess up, you can never change the way He loves you and wants to guide you to your destiny.

Don't miss out on your harvest by defining yourself by your past.

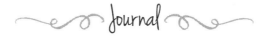

Journal

Sometimes we allow shame to sabotage the opportunities of the present. We feel unworthy based on our past issues and failures and therefore find ways to undermine or delay what God wants to do in our lives. Maybe it's "accidentally on purpose" being late for the job interview you know you really want. It could be sharing more than you need to share too soon in a new relation-ship. Sometimes it's reverting back to old habits and addictions for the kind of familiar relief that's no longer there.

It takes courage to move forward and receive all that God has for you. He has forgiven you and wants to bless you. But you have to forgive yourself and allow yourself to be surprised by the abun-dance of all He has for you. Sometimes we're the biggest obstacle to our own success. Sometimes we simply have to get out of the way and make room for God to work in our lives.

What are you most ashamed of? Why?

What one decision in your past do you wish you could change? What are the ongoing consequences of the mistake you made?

How has your shame changed you?

How can you use what broke you to help others?

I know I am not the only one who has ever experienced this shame, but still I can't move past this moment in my head. I can't stop judging myself about what happened. God, please take these thoughts and these memories and show me how I can learn from the things that broke me. Amen.

10

Surpass Them All

The one who gets counted out, talked about, and discredited can surpass them all.

Then she said, "I have found favor in your sight, my lord, for you have comforted me and indeed have spoken kindly to your maidservant, though I am not like one of your maidservants."

At mealtime Boaz said to her, "Come here, that you may eat of the bread and dip your piece of bread in the vinegar." So she sat beside the reapers; and he served her roasted grain, and she ate and was satisfied and had some left.

Ruth 2:13–14 NASB

A part of me always wanted to be a serious athlete. I love the commitment and discipline athletes put into their training. The sheer drive to push yourself to fulfill your maximum physical potential and the willpower to remain devoted to a goal day in and day out intrigue me. My only problem is that this part of me is so small compared with the part that hates working out. Sure, I feel great afterward, I like the way I look, and my clothes fit better. But in the moment, I *hate* summoning the energy and making my body work so much harder than it wants. I mean, no one enjoys pain, do they?

Maybe that's why I enjoy being a "couch coach" so much.

A couch coach is someone who sits at home on their couch and yells through the TV to coach their favorite athletes and teams. It's a vicarious way of bonding with my favorite athletes and teams and making my contribution, even if they never hear my instructions or know about my support. And how exciting it is when my favorite Olympian performs the way I wanted them to or my team pulls an upset! Honestly, though, I don't really know that much about sports, but every now and then I do get lucky.

One year we were all watching the Olympics as a family, and we decided to try to guess the winners. I was on a pretty impressive streak until it was time for the track-and-field events. After briefly leaving the room, I returned just as a new race started, so I picked the obvious choice—the runner currently in the lead. After all, I really had no other data to go on, right?

The timer was ticking and fans were erupting with cheers for the love of country and sports. Then I noticed a speck on the television screen. Way in the distant background of the track, something was moving crazy fast. It came closer and closer into the camera range until I realized it was another runner. Gaining momentum and speed, within minutes he was battling for the number-one spot. He came out of nowhere yet surpassed them all.

Talk about a come-from-behind victory for an underdog! This guy's speed was more than matched by his determination. Others may have doubted his talent or timing, but something deep down inside him knew that he had what it took to win the race. These victories inspire us all and remind us that no matter how far behind we may feel, there's still time to get ahead.

Ruth knew what it was like to come from behind before moving ahead. Gleaning the fields behind the paid reapers, she likely had been judged and dismissed with an eye roll and was merely being tolerated by them. It wasn't long, however, before Ruth found herself enjoying dinner with Boaz, the owner of the land.

Considering nothing but the objective facts on paper, Ruth may have been the least likely candidate for such an honor: a Moabite, a poor widow, someone with a commitment to care for an elderly relative, a woman who would always stand out from the natives there in Bethlehem. But Ruth went from being the least likely to advance in life to the only one to win Boaz's attention and, eventually, his heart.

The one they had counted out had now surpassed them all.

The scars we've received were never meant to dissuade us from living. Although our past mistakes can be the best prediction for our future, it's not because we are likely to repeat them, but because we can learn through them.

My scars taught me what to do *next time*—to use wisdom next time, to be afraid next time. Like Ruth's was, my life is certainly a mess on paper, but it is a beautiful piece of paper full of color that can only come from living. Each mark on my history serves as a reminder of how God found me. There were many dark days, many days when I felt like it would take me forever to catch up with my peers.

When the task seemed too daunting, I began pointing out all the reasons why this underdog couldn't win. My peers had never been divorced. They had no children. They didn't understand what it was like to grow up in church. Their parents had more time to help them than my parents' busy lifestyle would allow. I came up with plenty of excuses to never enter the race because I thought that failure was inevitable.

It's easy to talk ourselves out of living and instead settle comfortably on the couch, content coaching others to pursue their dreams while letting our own die. Each day we wake up, but before the day can get started we lull our ambition to sleep. We tell ourselves that even though we have the passion to win we don't have the potential. But it's never too late to reawaken your passion.

Finally, I determined I no longer wanted to be that person. When God so clearly had use of me, I could no longer count myself out.

The hardest part of accepting that I have a ministry was that I never felt usable. I didn't think God used people like me. But as I began to study, I learned that some of the stories we teach our children before they can even open the Bible are about broken people who dared to be used. God dares to use the broken because no one sees them anymore. And there's no attack like one you don't see coming.

It's not too late. It may look like you're behind now. It may appear to others that you won't be able to become much or accomplish anything. But God has seen your work. He has seen your dedication to fighting back against life's blows. Don't be tricked into believing that, if others don't endorse you, God can't use you. In His infinite wisdom and grace, He has no need to get approval from others to bless you.

Keep running, and do whatever it takes to stay in the race. Push yourself to go to class and finish your degree. Channel your energy into saving enough money to start your own business. Don't settle for an unhealthy relationship when you long for so much more. You may feel like there's no way you could ever achieve your dreams or make up for lost time. And you're right—you can't. But God can!

You may be toward the back of the pack, but the race isn't over yet.

Journal

We are encouraged to compare ourselves and compete in almost every area of life. Advertisements and commercials try to convince us that we need their special product in order to keep up with the Joneses and demonstrate our success. Exclusive clubs, corporations, committees, and, yes, even churches cater to an elite group who meet certain criteria—looks, career, clothes, status, spouse, kids, you name it. Even when we know we don't want to be part of such an elitist bunch, it's hard not to feel like we're losing life's race sometimes.

This is when we must remember that we're competing with no one but ourselves. Or, to phrase it the way God's Word describes it, we're running the race of faith so that we can persevere and fulfill the divine purpose for which we were created (see Hebrews 12:1). We don't have to be anyone else or beat anyone else. We simply have to keep taking the next step and then the next toward the collision with destiny awaiting us.

Do you feel like you're behind in your progress compared with others?

Are you giving your best effort to win the race, or has life taken away your endurance?

Ruth humbly gathered what was left over from the ladies who gleaned ahead of her. It wasn't ideal, but it was what she had to do to survive. She didn't allow pride to stand in her way. Can God trust you with your current position?

What do you need to do today to stay in the race?

 Prayer

Please allow me to see that even when I'm not where I want to be, I am exactly where You need me to be. I pray that I can accept when it's time for me to stay behind, and trust You when You take me higher. Most importantly, God, no matter what my current position may be, give me the strength to endure this race. Amen.

11

There Will Be an Overflow

Before, Ruth was gleaning whatever was left behind; now she had more than enough.

And when she rose up to glean, Boaz commanded his young men, saying, "Let her glean even among the sheaves, and do not reproach her. Also let grain from the bundles fall purposely for her; leave it that she may glean, and do not rebuke her."

Ruth 2:15–16 NKJV

Like most women, I enjoy shopping for new clothes. A little retail therapy can make your day brighter—as long as there's room for it in your budget. It would be great to buy some shoes, a couple nice bags, and a few outfits to match instead of paying bills. But the clothes do us no good if we don't have a home to store them, lights to see them, or water to wash them. So we learn to cut back on our wants and focus on our needs.

This isn't always easy in the heat of the moment—such as during a sale with 25 percent off! We can let our emotions control our decisions and end up feeling good for maybe a few minutes. But eventually, reality catches up with us when the credit card bill or bank statement comes. Then we only end up regretting our purchase and feeling more deprived than ever. Which—you guessed it—sets us up to repeat the process all over again.

It isn't necessarily our emotions that need to be controlled—in fact, we need to find a way to express what we're feeling when going through hard times. However, in the midst of those emotional moments, we do have to control our actions and make decisions that further our goals for complete healing rather than provide temporary bandages of relief.

Many times we only shop—or eat or gossip or work late—in order to indulge in a fantasy and escape the pain of our current reality. Some indulgences might numb the pain momentarily or shift the focus to something that feels good—like the taste of strawberry ice cream or the way a new silk blouse feels. But when used for escape instead of true enjoyment, any new focal point can quickly become one more obstacle on the road to success.

Instead we must focus on what we do have rather than what we don't. I've found that one of the best ways to balance my feelings when faced with decisions about how to proceed is to be grateful for what I have.

When I start complaining about the areas of lack in my life, I always remember one of my favorite Scriptures: "You have been faithful over a few things, I will make you ruler over many things" (Matthew 25:23 NKJV). You can't be faithful with what you have if you're always thinking about what you wish you had. We must strive to show God that we can be trusted with both blessings and struggles. Without trials, we could not fully appreciate our blessings. Ultimately, we value what we must work for.

When Ruth first came to the fields, she started gleaning behind the other ladies. What they had overlooked or been too full to carry became hers. Sure, it may not have been as much as they had, but it was hers. Once again, Ruth proves to us there's blessing in persevering. She refused to let the odds dictate her future. Boaz then ordered not only that she be allowed to glean with the other women but that they leave handfuls of grain for her.

It had to be humbling to stoop down and pick up what others had left behind. It may have been embarrassing to be in such a position. But Ruth had a priority that was bigger than any momentary shame or discomfort. Simply put, she and Naomi had to eat! Ruth knew she had to focus on the basics and didn't pretend otherwise.

When you're in a desperate place, there's no room for saving face! Now, don't get me wrong. As we see in Ruth's example, when times are hard, we still must do what we can do. We can't just become a victim of circumstance and wait for a handout that may never come.

This truth reminds me of the common saying, "God helps those who help themselves." While certainly a lot depends on the context, this adage reminds us that we have to do our part in order for God to do His. He can't help us if we're not willing to open our hands and pick up the grain that's right in front of us. It might not seem like enough or be what we prefer in that moment, but it still provides the sustenance we need. When we're willing to accept and use what we're given today, God takes notice and leads us on a path toward abundance tomorrow.

Our God is a God of more than enough. He won't just bless you; He'll blow your mind. Will you let Him?

Boaz directed his servants to give Ruth special treatment. Before he noticed her, she was gleaning whatever was left behind; now she had more than enough. Ruth went from wondering what she and Naomi would eat that day to experiencing abundance.

As God did for Ruth, we can trust that He will see we've been faithful and can be trusted with overflow. When God promotes you, He's going to give you special treatment. Where you once struggled, now you will have abundance.

God is waiting to create an overflow in your areas of lack. Before He can bless you, though, He must know that He can trust you. Be grateful for what you have. Sure, we all have areas in our lives that we wish we could improve, but we can't afford to invest in worry. Make the best out of what you do have; then let God do the rest.

Journal

When I was dating my husband in college, we moved in with each other. We struggled financially for a while until I finally got a job as a receptionist; almost a year after that he was drafted into the NFL. Our financial lack was over, but we were lacking in more areas than we could see at the time.

We thought our biggest struggle was becoming financially stable. Once that was no longer an issue, it became evident that we were lacking emotionally more severely than I thought. I was so focused on not having overflow in the area I wanted that I ignored the places that needed it the most. Our self-esteem, confidence in one another, and self-love were nonexistent. We had an overflow of finances, but without emotional stability we also had an overflow of passion, pain, women, and verbal abuse.

You may not be where you want to be, but if you want God to bless you, you have to give Him permission to work in the area He chooses. Trust God will give you the desires of your heart when your heart and mind are ready to receive them.

Identify the areas of lack in your life.

Have you shown yourself to be faithful over those areas in your life?

Have you ever been trusted with overflow (extra money, time, freedom)? How did you handle it?

Ruth did *everything* she could to survive. Are you using all of whatever you have left from your despair to make tomorrow a better day? What could you be doing differently?

God, help me not to dwell on the pain that I felt, the tears I cried, or the memories that won't fade. Lord, only You can take my not enough and turn it into more than I ever imagined. So here I am, God, turning it over to You. I don't know what You can do with these pieces, but I know it's better than anything I could do. Amen.

12

Make Others Believe

Your ability to keep the faith, despite all that has happened, will help others believe.

So she gleaned in the field until evening. Then she beat out what she had gleaned, and it was about an ephah of barley. She took it up and went into the city, and her mother-in-law saw what she had gleaned. She also took it out and gave Naomi what she had left after she was satisfied.

Her mother-in-law then said to her, "Where did you glean today and where did you work? May he who took notice of you be blessed." So she told her mother-in-law with whom she had worked and said, "The name of the man with whom I worked today is Boaz." Naomi said to her daughter-in-law, "May he be blessed of the Lord who has not withdrawn his kindness to the living and to the dead." Again Naomi said to her, "The man is our relative, he is one of our closest relatives."

Ruth 2:17–20 NASB

The first time I had to speak at my home church, I was beyond nervous. Many of the congregants in our church had been firsthand witnesses to every collision in my life. I questioned whether the people who had seen me at my worst would be able to receive my best.

I felt the butterflies in my stomach anytime anyone said a word that started with a W; it was a constant reminder that Wednesday Night Bible Study was just weeks away. I studied and prayed, and then asked God to have His way before His people. When the evening came, the whole time I was speaking, I could hear my mother even though I couldn't see her. Her reassuring "Amens" comforted me. I knew she wanted me to know I wasn't alone.

It humbled me to see how many people were blessed by the message God had given me to share, but finally seeing my mother was priceless. Her face held the same expression it does when she sees my father speaking. She told me I blessed her. Somehow, even though she knew every shameful secret in my closet, she saw that I'd fallen unapologetically in love with the God in me. I'm not sure if she truly realizes that she taught me the power of falling in love with God. Parenting is a beautiful training course in which adults protect their children and teach them what to do when they feel most unprotected. How they handle their own misdirection will teach their children what to do when they're lost themselves.

As a child, I took so much for granted. My parents provided not only the material things—food, clothing, shelter—but the essential ones that make a house a home: love, forgiveness, laughter, security. The older I became, the more I realized that I was so blessed to have parents who loved each other and loved their children in ways that made their sacrifices seem effortless.

It wasn't until I reached adulthood that I understood the impact of parenting. More than the family vacations or the stories before bed, my most treasured memories of my parents were the things they didn't say. The generational core values of who I am weren't instilled through verbal communication. I watched them, and watching them taught me.

As their own parents aged, I watched my father and mother care, guide, and protect my grandparents all the way to their final stages of life. It is the most profound memory for me because it taught me that the true sign of gratitude is service. My parents showed their appreciation for the sacrifices their parents had made by serving them when they could no longer help themselves.

I now try to show my parents my own gratitude in whatever small ways I can. Whether it's cooking dinner, running errands, or pulling back their covers for bed, I try to show them what I have witnessed: Anytime God blesses them, they serve in return. I like surprising them with the same kinds of kindnesses that they have done for me my entire life.

Naomi was convinced God had cursed her. When God blessed Ruth, it helped Naomi to believe again. When Ruth was finished gleaning, she took what she had accrued and shared it with Naomi. When Naomi saw that Ruth's faithfulness had been rewarded, she dared to believe again. Maybe God had not forgotten her after all. Ruth's blessing helped Naomi's joy return.

After all the people in her life that she had lost, it's no wonder that Naomi became bitter and wondered how she would continue with her life. When one loss leads to another and another, it's hard to hope even when new opportunities blossom. But God clearly did not abandon Naomi because Ruth remained committed to her mother-in-law beyond obligation. She loved the older woman like a mother and wanted to be the conduit for Naomi to hope again.

Inspiring someone brings such a different feeling than making a friend, connecting with them intellectually, or being able to make them laugh does. When you inspire someone, it means something you said or did made him or her want to be better. When we are young, our heroes are often celebrities—athletes, actors, music stars. We admire the talent and success of these individuals and want to emulate certain qualities they possess. As we mature, though, we begin to realize that the true heroes of life are often right in front of us: parents, brothers and sisters, teachers and pastors, coaches and mentors. The people we get to see every day can inspire us in ways that celebrities never can. Most importantly, they model what it means to persevere, to live by faith, and to turn trials into triumph.

Ruth was just trying to survive. She had once pledged her life and love to her husband, Mahlon. Even after his death, she was committed to making sure what was left of him, through her relationship with Naomi, was nurtured. Ruth decided she would do whatever it took to survive the challenges that come with making that commitment. Maybe it was even easier for her to search for food, pick up the leftover grain, and accept the kindness of Boaz because she wasn't doing it just for herself. Ruth knew that whatever affected her would affect Naomi. When we love someone, we do whatever it takes to push through obstacles and provide all that we can.

Who knows why God chose you to bear the weight that you do. But perhaps you aren't struggling just for you. Your ability to remain faithful in spite of pain can help someone—but only if you show them. Don't be so obsessed with an image of perfection that you miss an opportunity to show where grace abides in your life. You never know whom you might inspire—or when they might in turn inspire you.

Journal

Growing up in the church, I often saw people desperate for hope. They might have been dealing with a serious illness, a painful relationship, a financial crisis, or just the toll of everyday life, but they knew that what they needed was more than just physical or emotional healing. When they experienced the compassion, care, and concern of others in our community, the kindness they experienced nourished a hope that life could be different, which they in turn soon passed on to others hungry for hope.

This is church at its best, when people can rally around one another and provide the kind of support and encouragement that inspires us to be the best version of ourselves. This is how God allows us to be Christ to one another.

How has your life been affected by the sacrifices of those around you?

Do you let the success or failures of your family and friends inspire you or intimidate you?

How have you shown others what God has done in your life?

How could sharing your testimony protect someone who hears you?

Prayer

Lord, if I knew my story could spare someone from what I experienced, I would share it with Your people. I'm just so afraid of being judged and criticized. God, give me the wisdom not to throw my pearls among swine. Instead, allow me to save them and share them with those who can see the worth in my struggle. Amen.

13

Extra Protection

Not only will God bless you, but He will protect you along with the blessing He's entrusted to you.

Then Ruth the Moabite said, "He even said to me, 'Stay with my workers until they finish harvesting all my grain.'"

Naomi said to Ruth her daughter-in-law, "It will be good for you, my daughter, to go with the women who work for him, because in someone else's field you might be harmed."

So Ruth stayed close to the women of Boaz to glean until the barley and wheat harvests were finished. And she lived with her mother-in-law.

Ruth 2:21–23

The Secret Service has many responsibilities. Among them is protecting the president, vice president, their families, cabinet members, and other designated individuals. Recently, Congress passed a law that allows former presidents to have Secret Service protection for life. As the world seems to become increasingly more dangerous, I see why it is necessary to provide lifetime security to those who were elected to the highest office in government, even after they leave the White House. Their elevated status remains even when their time in office has ended.

Just like we see with such political figures, when God elevates us, He also protects us. He does not promote us to new positions of responsibility and blessing as a setup for a takedown. God's protection ensures that we can continue to grow and develop as stewards of the abundant life we've been given.

Boaz had given Ruth unprecedented access to his fields. Within one day she went from gleaning what was left over to having more than enough. In addition, Boaz made sure not only that she received plenty of grain but that she would not be harmed or threatened. Ruth did not have to worry about losing her gifts by being attacked, robbed, raped, or disrespected. Boaz was her protector as well as her provider.

This passage of Ruth reminds us that God doesn't bless us without protecting us. Too often we believe we're ready for our blessing, but when we receive it, we instantly become afraid of losing it. As if God may not bless us more than once, we allow fear to make us stingy. We must remember that He doesn't provide for us and bless us today only to pull it all away from us tomorrow. He gives us the protection we need to maintain our blessings.

The same God who protected Ruth and Naomi as they journeyed from Moab to Bethlehem was with them when He elevated them from just enough to overflow. His protection and blessings run parallel. He is our good Father who delights in giving His children good gifts.

Do not let the insecurity that something could be taken away cause you to hold too tightly to an object and, ultimately, let go of God. Similarly, sometimes we may need to let go of what He has given us so that He can enlarge our blessing and give us even more. Remember, He has promised that if we serve Him—not things or people—no weapon formed against us shall prosper.

The day I signed my name on the dotted line of my book contract, I wondered if I had what it takes to produce "author quality" work. Even though the publisher approached me because of my blog, I wondered if they realized I had just "stumbled" into writing.

I had two manuscripts down when I accepted that God was certainly the ink behind my pen. Praise started pouring in about my memoir *Lost and Found*. "I have a feeling this is going to be big!" everyone said. After hearing that the tenth time, I started doubting myself again. Did I have the ideas and creativity to truly present my life to the world in a way that felt safe?

We all see our favorite magazines and television shows enthralled with introducing a new voice to the nation. But often, if a newcomer to the spotlight lacks preparation, we also get to view the many struggles they must face while they find their way. I didn't want to be that person who got an opportunity their character wasn't prepared for.

So I prayed. I asked God to bring people into my life who could help me be who He created me to be. I wanted Him to remove distractions and give me grace to create innovative methods to reach new hearts for Him. I had to fight for the right to be heard. I had to fight for the ideas that no one believed in. I had to take a chance on myself and trust that God wouldn't give me this promotion if He didn't provide protection.

I formulated my ideas, did research, and presented them nervously to a room of professionals who'd worked on more books than I'd ever read. They loved every concept, every marketing idea, every social media strategy. Perhaps I "stumbled" into a book deal, but I didn't really stumble into writing. I just walked into what God had already predestined for my life.

God doesn't give us favor without protection. If He trusted you enough to give it to you, He'll provide the security it requires to guard His investment. Don't become stingy or greedy. Instead, remember, "He who began a good work in you will carry it on to completion until the day of Christ Jesus" (Philippians 1:6).

Journal

I once saw an episode of *Oprah* about a mother who couldn't get out of depression after burying her child. Who could blame her? I buzzed around the house with the TV on waiting to hear what wisdom Dr. Phil would provide. He basically told the heartbroken mother that focusing on the moment of death was a disservice to the time her daughter did have. And while I can't compare my detours to losing a child, I know that many times I focused so much on the losses in my life that I didn't cherish what the loss gave me. How can we lose and gain at the same time? By making the loss serve our future.

What is the most valuable thing you have ever lost?

How has your perspective on the loss changed over time?

How would your life be different if you had never experienced this loss?

Have you allowed what you lost to make you better or bitter?

God, help me to see that everything I've lost helped make me better. It may have hurt, and I may have been broken. But I know that if You saw fit for me to lose now, it's so that I can win later. Help me to believe You still see me. I truly want to live again, but I'm scared. I'm afraid of losing again. I need to believe You'll protect all that You have invested in me. Amen.

14

The Beginning of the End

We must dedicate ourselves to gathering the left-overs and keeping the faith, knowing that if God did it for her, He'll do it for us.

Blessed be he of the Lord, who has not forsaken His kindness to the living and the dead!"

Ruth 2:20 NKJV

Have you ever run into an old friend—at the mall or church or even a class reunion—and not recognized her? You know she looks familiar and that you probably do know her, but she's clearly not the same as she once was. Then you see it—the smile in her eyes where there once was fear, the joy in her laugh instead of a clenched jaw, or the warmth in her hug rather than a polite pat. It's clear that more has changed than just her makeup, hairstyle, and taste in fashion. Something has come alive and flourished in your friend's spirit. She's found her place in the world. You might even be tempted to envy her.

Maybe you went through a hard time together in the past, but it's clear that your friend came out stronger and more confident. Or maybe it was just a matter of her discovering what she was good at in her career, or finding a man who loved her, or becoming a parent. Regardless of what caused the changes, it's clear that your friend has become a better version of herself, a more authentic woman engaged with the art of living.

I wonder sometimes if Ruth's old friends back in Moab would have recognized her if they saw her scrutinizing the ground for kernels of left-behind wheat. I wonder if they would have believed the rumors that her new neighbors were spreading about her. And

I wonder if they ever could have imagined her relationship and marriage to Boaz.

In the beginning of chapter 2, we meet a dedicated Ruth, determined to keep her faith as well as her commitment to her mother-in-law. When the chapter ends, Ruth is on the verge of a breakthrough. After the devastation of losing the men in her life, traveling to a new city, facing gossip, trying to take care of Naomi, and struggling with discouragement, she finds her fate changing quickly. As her trials come to an end, she learns there are blessings waiting for her and protection covering her.

This second chapter is my favorite in the book of Ruth. Within twenty-three verses, Ruth's life begins to turn completely around. This chapter relates the events that seem like the turning point in her story. She went from a mindset of simply surviving to an unexpected collision with destiny. How could she have known that the tears she cried, the weight she carried, and the rumors spread about her were all just preparation? How could she have known that what was taken away was simply making room for what was to come?

When life becomes too much to bear, it's easy to become despondent. Our fears smother us with worries and regret. We can't imagine ever being carefree and joyful again. We're tempted to obsess about what we've lost and allow our bitterness to fester. We become stagnant and don't know how to get out of the ditch where life seems to have left us.

But this is the very time we must dedicate ourselves to gathering the leftovers and keeping the faith. We must choose to believe that if God did it for Ruth, He'll do it for us. We can come out of the storm. The torrential rain will turn to a slow drizzle. Thunder may rumble, but only as a distant echo of the danger it once threatened.

After dropping out of college, I started working as a waitress at an adult club. I knew that if people from church could see me, they'd be so ashamed. I worked there for as long as I could, but when my mother found out, I knew I had to quit. I didn't want her to be ashamed of me, but I needed to make ends meet.

Within a few weeks of quitting waitressing, I landed a job with an air force contractor. I knew nothing about the military. Outside of tutoring and the strip club, I'd never held a real job. I wasn't sure if I would be good at it. I was supposed to be a junior in college by now; instead I was learning terms about weaponry and different routes into Iraq. It was honest work, though.

My life wasn't going as planned, but I was surviving the best I knew how. I wouldn't be able to give my parents the satisfaction of watching me walk across the stage to get my bachelor's degree. But maybe I could discover something inside of me that would make them just as proud. I was just picking up the pieces from the mess I had made, but I see now that God was with me even when I felt most unworthy of His presence.

Keep holding on to His promise and see what's next for you.

That thing that hurts you, the people you lost along the way, and the moments when you decided to push instead of giving up are all preparation. Look over your life—the choices you made and the shame you feel may never go away. Aren't you ready to see what God can do? Then just keep walking, step-by-step, day-by-day.

Ruth's commitment to walk with God is the only reason she was on course to collide with destiny. Collisions hurt. They cause injuries and create pain, but the insurance that comes with God reminds us that everything that was damaged can be restored and replaced. Whether God is just making a few minor repairs in your life or totaling out your dreams so you can experience His will, don't shy away from the pain of collision.

As Ruth learned, it may be the only way you discover your destiny.

Journal

The book of Ruth begins with death, but by the end of chapter 2 we see obvious signs of new life. Not only did Ruth lose her husband, and Naomi her husband and two sons, but both women also lost the world as they knew it. When their loved ones died, so did their expectations for how their lives would proceed. Everything changed, and it wasn't clear how things would look when the dust settled.

Both Ruth and Naomi had to grieve all that they had lost—a part of themselves—or risk being consumed by their pain. In order for new life to emerge from the ashes, we must be willing to go through a period when the ground of our heart remains fallow. We must bury the old dreams that can no longer come to pass in order for new ones to be planted and take root.

What has to die in your life so that you can live?

Death brings grief and grief brings pain. Birth brings new life, but it also brings pain. How are you using your pain? Are you creating something new or still grieving what could have been?

If things turned around for you overnight, what would your pain have taught you that you will never forget?

Write a letter about your darkest pain. Write about how it affected your life. Describe any regret or shame you carried.

Imagine yourself free from the feelings you wrote about. Healed from the pain that haunts you. What does that girl look like? How has she become better? What makes her smile?

You can be that girl. You are on the road to a better you. Just like Ruth, your willingness to open your heart means you're on the verge of a breakthrough.

Prayer

God, thank You for this breaking. Thank You for the pain and the tears. I'm thankful because You trusted me with this pain, grateful because here I am now, looking back and thanking You. Lord, I'm asking You to use these broken pieces to make me better. Help me to become wiser and stronger. I don't know what's in store for me, but I know I don't want to do it without You. Amen.

15

It's Time to Try Again

*There will be moments after hurt and heartache
when we must make the decision to try again.*

One day Naomi said to Ruth, "My daughter, it's time that I found a permanent home for you, so that you will be provided for. Boaz is a close relative of ours, and he's been very kind by letting you gather grain with his young women. Tonight he will be winnowing barley at the threshing floor. Now do as I tell you—take a bath and put on perfume and dress in your nicest clothes. Then go to the threshing floor, but don't let Boaz see you until he has finished eating and drinking. Be sure to notice where he lies down; then go and uncover his feet and lie down there. He will tell you what to do."

Ruth 3:1–4 NLT

My mother underwent knee surgery, and as part of her recovery, she spent a few days in the hospital's rehabilitation facility. While visiting her there, I overheard a physical trainer telling another patient, a recent amputee, that the only way he would learn to use his prosthesis was if he tried. Evidently, the patient had been refusing to attempt to walk for some time. The trainer's frustration was beginning to show as he realized the hospital would eventually send the patient home if he continued to refuse his rehabilitation.

Instantly, I thought of my first real heartbreak and how hard it was for me to dare loving again. There are some pains so deep that we never want to try again. When you lose a part of yourself, it's hard to imagine you can continue to live as if something isn't missing. Sure, the patient's leg had been replaced with a prosthetic that would allow him to function, but he had to make the decision to try again.

It's one thing to be afraid of the unknown; it's another for our known experiences to inhibit us. You see, the patient didn't hate his prosthetic. He wasn't afraid of his trainer. The recovery work wasn't what made him despondent. The patient couldn't even fully evaluate those things because he couldn't escape the memory of what had hurt him and what he had lost.

Having worked on many cases, the trainer knew something the patient did not. If the patient dares to try, he learns that a prosthetic can become just as functional as his lost limb. It doesn't diminish the loss, but it does allow him to move forward. It's a choice of the will to illuminate the darkness of grief with a spark of hope.

These moments are when the real seeds of our future are planted. No matter how devastating our loss, how excruciating our pain, or how challenging our circumstances may be, we always have choices. They may be limited, they may not be the decisions we want to face, but we still get to choose how we will respond to life. We aren't animals that simply react on instinct in order to survive. We have a spirit inside us that is divinely created and inspired.

Naomi's faith was restored because of Ruth's commitment to survival. In exchange, Naomi wanted to remind Ruth that the time had come for her to be restored, too. We've seen Ruth do what she could do by securing leftover grain so that they could make flour and bread. But now Naomi is doing what she can do by sharing her wisdom as an older female with her daughter. Naomi has clearly thought through a plan of action, not to entrap or seduce Boaz with Ruth's charms, but to simply provide an opportunity for them to speak privately.

In their culture, it was rare that a man and a woman who were not related would be alone together, unless they were to be married—and then, usually only by arrangement of their families. But since Ruth was a widow without a patriarch to arrange a marriage for her, Naomi came up with a way that would still allow the younger woman to have direct access to Boaz. They already knew he was a good man with a generous, compassionate heart, so they were not worried that he would take advantage of the situation or disrespect Ruth in any way. Once again, their circumstances seemed to limit their choices and actions, but Naomi finally seemed to have moved beyond her bitterness to a new place, a place of hope and possibility.

They had both been devastated, but notice that hidden within the word *devastate* is the word *state*. If you've ever driven coast to coast across our country, you know you have to go through a lot of states. When we go through a state of heartbreak, it's important for us to remember that our condition was not meant to keep us from reaching our divine destination.

Do not make devastation your permanent dwelling place. Instead, allow it to be a temporary place on your journey to recovery. The only way to escape your state of pain is to move. It's time to try again. Just as the patient must choose whether or not to allow the pain of what happened to keep him from trying, you, too, must decide whether to be constrained by agony or propelled by hope.

It's not easy. It's not comfortable. It's not something you can ignore.

But it's still a choice.

Journal

When Ruth had to start over with Naomi, she had to make several adjustments along the way. Through it all, she also learned many things about herself. She learned to do with less. Through keeping her commitment to Naomi, she learned she had character. Her dedication to gleaning the leftovers showed her humility. If you look back and focus on something other than the pain, you'll see you're wiser and stronger now than you were before.

List three positive things you learned about yourself through your pain.

How have those lessons changed your outlook on life?

What are some small changes you can make now to help continue the starting-over process?

Prayer

Lord, help me to see that I have the strength to try again. I may have been hurt, but I am stronger than I was before. I don't want my pain to be in vain. I want to use these lessons to reach my destiny. Clear my mind so that I can quiet the doubts and fears of my past. I want to be free when You say it's time to try again. Amen.

16

Respect Those Who Came Before You

There is wisdom for your journey in listening to the wise counsel of others.

And she said to her, "All that you say to me I will do." So she went down to the threshing floor and did according to all that her mother-in-law instructed her.

Ruth 3:5–6 NKJV

'm at the age where I now realize that most of my parents' advice, comments, and guidance have been right all along. It's been a slow journey that began when I was a child, veered off track when I was a teenager, and has returned to the illumination of their wisdom as I've entered adulthood. More times than not, when my parents tried to warn me I was playing with fire, it wasn't until my skin was scorched that I conceded they were right.

Finally tired of receiving burns, I started listening. It didn't just stop there, though; the people whose opinions I once ignored have become the ones I now often seek out. When I first decided to purchase a home, I presented my plans to both my mom and dad. I wanted their advice on whether I was thinking things through clearly or needed to make some changes. I didn't want them to tell me what to do, but I needed them to share their wisdom gleaned from experience.

So much of growing and maturing has to do with the process, and not just the end result. Especially as a grown woman, I don't want my parents or anyone else to tell me what to do or which direction to take. Yet I welcome their input, their suggestions, their advice, and their counsel—particularly as it's drawn from their own experience. They can't tell me what decisions to make or how to live my life, but they can influence me with their own battle-worn wisdom.

God places in our lives people who know us and love us enough to tell us the truth. Even if the truth makes us uncomfortable or upset, we mustn't ignore the words of the wise. Wisdom comes through experience, and experience through living. Why deny the opportunity to take a small peek into the future by ignoring the advice of those who went before you? Certainly, we all have our own struggles and mistakes to make, but ultimately we can spare ourselves a lot of trouble by simply listening.

My generation is largely responsible for the skyrocket in social networking. We didn't give a second thought to posting photos, updating our friends on the day, and commenting on others' posts. Our parents, however, didn't understand the phenomenon at all. Initially, that is.

It took a few years, but as social networking started rising in popularity, so did our parents' interest. They went from not understanding why we'd want to tell our world every small detail in our lives to peeking casually over our shoulders as we scrolled our page. "What's that?" my mother finally asked. I smiled on the inside as my mother's resistance began to gradually decrease.

Most of my friends had similar experiences with their parents. Eventually, usually without warning, they all started receiving friend requests from their parents. Suddenly our parents were reconnecting with their classmates, neighbors, and long-lost family members. They began to learn the benefits, and drawbacks, of our secret social pleasures.

And though we all complained a bit, and murmured some, I believe our parents' presence on social networks created boundaries for us. Those boundaries were necessary. It taught us to not be impulsive and to think before posting. Conversely, I believe that we showed them how to see the world—and how others view it—from the palm of your hand.

Surely our balance could have been achieved had we simply listened to our parents when they first initiated their questions. But sometimes we're afraid that opening ourselves up to counsel will mean we have to follow their directions or risk disappointing them. We should be open to seeing our lives through another view. It's not a mandate to follow exactly, but it is another perspective.

Sometimes all we need is a little perspective.

Listening and integrating what we hear into our own experiences not only produces wisdom but allows it to seep into our own lives. When we know others are for our good, we can take the gifts they offer and make them part of our consideration process. We respect their ability to survive and to learn whenever we assimilate what they've shared into our own journey.

On the way from Moab back to Bethlehem, Naomi told Ruth not to stay with her. The older woman tried to convince her daughter-in-law that life would be much easier if she returned to her homeland. Ruth listened, then made a decision for herself. Their circumstances changed, and once again Naomi gave Ruth advice—but this time Ruth listened and heeded what she heard. Naomi didn't decide to stop giving advice just because Ruth didn't take it previously. Naomi respected Ruth's right to make a decision about her life, even if she didn't agree with it.

Even if we have not always agreed with or heeded the advice we've been given in the past, we can, like Ruth, still welcome the input of those special individuals who care about us with the best of intentions. The choice remains ours and ours alone, but knowing someone else has traveled the same route or experienced the same feelings can make a huge difference. If nothing else, we realize that we're not alone. We will survive. We can get through this and back on track in the pursuit of our divine destiny.

It's important that we take a moment to at least listen to those who are trying to help us. You don't have to follow their advice or agree with everything they say, but make the decision to let other trusted individuals challenge your thought process. If we are not challenged, we cannot learn.

Journal

I've observed a definite pattern in my life. Before many of my most important and best decisions, I have sought the counsel of significant people in my life. Similarly, before many of my most important and worst decisions, I did *not* seek advice from anyone. Well, that's not entirely true—I may have asked for advice but I didn't listen. You don't have to like what you hear or agree with everything that's said, but when people whom you trust and respect speak into your life, accept it as a priceless gift.

Name three people you truly respect.

How have you been influenced by their lives?

How will you use their influences on your own journey of self-discovery?

How can you use your story to help soothe or counsel someone who's hurt in the same way you are?

Prayer

God, ignite a light inside of me that will lead others to You. May my life be a representation of Your power to mend the broken. I pray that others look at my heart and see that Your light is capable of shining through the darkest of hurts. Thank You for allowing such strong people to go ahead of me so that I may use their shoulders to reach higher heights. Amen.

17

Be Vulnerable

There will be moments when others reveal their vulnerability and you're invited to let down your guard with them. We all need a place of shelter so that we can provide the same for others.

*W*hen Boaz had finished eating and drinking and was in good spirits, he went over to lie down at the far end of the grain pile. Ruth approached quietly, uncovered his feet and lay down. In the middle of the night something startled the man; he turned—and there was a woman lying at his feet!

"Who are you?" he asked.

"I am your servant Ruth," she said. "Spread the corner of your garment over me, since you are a guardian-redeemer of our family."

Ruth 3:7–9

The older my siblings and I have become, the more trust we've gained from our parents. There's something so strange and wonderful about having the people who once told you what to do occasionally ask you what *they* should do. The dynamic has changed from my parents always giving directions to their seeking and respecting my opinions.

It's an incredible gift to be trusted with the unguarded pieces of who a person really is. Especially when that person is someone you admire and emulate as your teacher or mentor. In these moments we have the opportunity to take the relationship to a new level of maturity by matching their vulnerability with our own.

When you risk being vulnerable by giving your opinions and relating to someone at peer level, there's always a chance it will complicate the relationship in uncomfortable ways. When each person reveals a deeper facet of their personality or true identity, there's a fear that the other might be surprised, offended, or unable to accept this part of us. On the other hand, these moments of self-revelation and reciprocal transparency forge a bond of intimacy that is pure and strong.

When Ruth went to lie at Boaz's feet, he was unguarded and vulnerable. After having a festive evening with plenty of drinks and merriment, he finally allowed himself to sleep. We're not told his age, but it seems safe to assume that he was an established man, perhaps nearing middle-age. Apparently, though, he had not married and started a family. Maybe he had not had the opportunity or his family had not arranged a marriage for him. Maybe he was a little bit of a romantic and wanted to wait until someone special wandered through his fields.

So imagine how startled he must have been to find Ruth lying at his feet. Don't you wonder what thoughts must have run through his mind? He didn't know who she was or what her intentions were. Was she a crazy stalker there to harm him or rob him? A wily seductress there to hop in his bed as the means by which to exploit his wealth? Or something else? A sincere woman in need of help?

And consider the risk Ruth was taking. After life robbed her of her plans, she had been forced to bury her husband, leave her hometown, and create a new life. Ruth had allowed survival to toughen her. Yet in this moment she matched Boaz's physical vulnerability with her emotional one. Tongues had already been wagging about her ever since she came to town. If word got out that she had sneaked into Boaz's place and hid by his bed until he went to sleep . . . well, they wouldn't need tabloids to create the kind of buzz such a discovery would ignite. Ruth would be confirmed as a gold digger, an opportunist, a foreign woman there to entrap her next husband.

But as we know—and as Boaz quickly found out—Ruth was not that kind of person.

She simply needed a refuge. She requested Boaz to take her under his wing. Like a baby bird unprepared to face the world alone, Ruth wanted Boaz to protect her.

This was an intimate moment of transparency for both of them. Boaz, a powerful businessman who appeared to have it all together, was caught physically defenseless. Ruth, a strong woman determined to survive and not be beaten down by life, admitted she was weary.

In a practical sense and not just my romantic imagination, they both needed each other. It made sense and seemed like the inevitable culmination after God had led them to each other. Their paths had crossed for a reason, and now they faced the turning point head on. After that night, things would never be the same between them again, one way or another.

These turning points must be recognized, respected, and cherished. As my siblings and I grew older, we began to spread our own wings. No longer in need of constant covering, we've matured enough to occasionally provide refuge for our parents. As my parents began to entrust us with the whispers of their hearts, we advanced from being just their children. We now get to provide a place of shelter and rest for them.

As this passage of Ruth demonstrates, everyone—no matter how strong or how weak—needs relationships in which they can rest and be vulnerable. Sure, you can cook dinner, do the laundry, punch the clock, take the classes, care for your parents, balance the checkbook, counsel your friends, and still have time to prepare for tomorrow. But every now and then, you must trust someone with the vulnerable side of you.

Remove the cape, take off the mask, and allow yourself to be human again. Yes, you can keep it moving. But you know a part of you is no longer strong enough to hold everything together. It's time to admit you need covering.

Journal

My best friend, Stacia, is five years older than I am. We've been best friends since I was fifteen. She is probably the one person who knows the most about me, and even the things she doesn't know, I must have forgotten to tell her.

It always upsets me when I hear people say that women can't get along. It's one of the reasons I believe in being so transparent. I believe at the core of our beings we all desire to live our best life, but often we are distracted by travesties that occur in our lives. Stacia and I have managed to remain best friends mostly by telephone. We've gone over a year without seeing each other, but still talked every day. Even in the absence of fun distractions like trips to the spa, movies, and girls' nights out, Stacia and I bonded over our words—those thoughts and emotions that we couldn't share with the people around us but could safely tell an ear a few hundred miles away.

Our friendship has taught me that when you become vulnerable, you can truly let a person in. Love is the only option. We're strong enough to be wrong, though. You have to give your heart enough credit. The vulnerability that exists with my best friend has encouraged us to be brave in our other relationships. We've learned to trust that God can heal any wounds we may endure in the quest of loving others and ourselves.

When you're upset, who's the one person who can calm you down?

What is it they do that relaxes you?

How has this relationship shaped how you handle other people when they're angry?

How are your actions when handling another's vulnerability a reflection of Christ's love?

Please teach me the balanced dance of grace and mercy. May I provide a flicker of hope in a person's darkest hour. I pray You give me the perfect wisdom to speak to the heart of the matter. And may I be as gentle with others as You have been with me. Amen.

18

Your Blessing Is in Your Obedience

Sometimes what you can do and what you should do are completely different.

Then he said, "May you be blessed of the Lord, my daughter. You have shown your last kindness to be better than the first by not going after young men, whether poor or rich. Now, my daughter, do not fear. I will do for you whatever you ask, for all my people in the city know that you are a woman of excellence. Now it is true I am a close relative; however, there is a relative closer than I. Remain this night, and when morning comes, if he will redeem you, good; let him redeem you. But if he does not wish to redeem you, then I will redeem you, as the Lord lives. Lie down until morning."

Ruth 3:10–13 NASB

Recently I was on this diet. Not sure which one, but I know I stayed hungry. I mean, technically I was eating enough, but I couldn't shake the notion that if something wasn't fried, it wasn't good. So I had thrown away anything in my house that could possibly tempt me to break my diet. Then one day, after spending the afternoon with their favorite aunt, my children returned home with McDonald's Happy Meals. Any other day I wouldn't have cared, but that day I had just seen a commercial for the fast-food chain and suddenly the nuggets looked delicious.

I wanted the taste but not the calories, so (don't judge me, okay?) I chewed the chicken nugget, just for the taste, and then spit it out. (You're judging. . . . Stop!) Sad, I know. Afterward, I especially appreciated why my trainer had told me to throw away all the junk food in my house. It's so much easier to be obedient when you don't have any other options. Temptations may still come—and they likely will—but you can give yourself a fighting chance by removing potential obstacles to your goals when you see them.

With a deceased husband and bitter mother-in-law, Ruth suddenly had plenty of options. She had at least a couple good reasons to go her own way and do whatever she pleased. And Boaz recognized that she had other options. Still, Ruth chose to obey the customs of her new land. Boaz commended her for keeping her commitment to her deceased husband even though he was no longer there to witness it.

Boaz also applauded the way she had demonstrated that she was a woman of "noble character." Ruth clearly had not taken the easy road, the path of least resistance, of staying back in her homeland and making the best of it. Instead, she had followed her heart and accompanied Naomi on an adventure that required stepping out in faith. Such a commitment obviously saddled Ruth with more responsibility and became a liability if finding a new husband was her main priority.

And even though the locals might have speculated about this stranger collecting grain for herself and her mother-in-law, eventually they saw no evidence to support criticism. She had not chased after other men—younger men—just so that she could have the security of a husband or the income to restore her lifestyle. No, Ruth had waited on the Lord's timing and had remained faithful day to day. Now, after taking perhaps the greatest risk of her life, her faith was being recognized and rewarded.

The true measure of a person is revealed when they have options. Do you tithe on your paycheck or buy an extra pair of shoes? Do you use your sphere of influence to help build up others or just to build up yourself? Do you act the same way when you travel for your job as you do at home?

Who are you when no one is watching?

We make life so much more difficult than it has to be, all because we make God an option instead of a priority. If you're going to continue to grow in Christ, you must remove from your life anything that will distract you from Him. Yes, it's good to have options, but not if they are distracting you from your destiny. You have to keep your eyes on the prize and remind yourself of what you really want and not just the McNugget in the moment!

The world allows us numerous opportunities to choose between our flesh and our God. We don't always choose correctly, but God is gracious enough to take all of our missteps and incorporate them into His master vision. Don't let a disobedient past prohibit you from having an ordained future. It's only on the road of obedience that we collide with our destiny—not when we're trailblazing off on our own.

When you do your part to discipline your decisions and align them with God's guidance, then you will be rewarded. It may not be on the timetable you want or expect, but the day will come when opportunity beckons you to the next level. Ruth is rewarded for her faithfulness in the small things as well as recognized for her integrity. The two go hand in hand—what you do reflects who you really are, and vice versa. Your character, values, and priorities shape your thinking and influence your actions.

Align the noble woman inside you with the desires of your heart and allow God to reveal what He has for you in His time. You are stronger than you realize. You are being redeemed by the ultimate Guardian-Redeemer.

Journal

Sometimes in my life, I didn't want to do the right thing. The thought of giving my best to a situation and not being truly sure how it all would pan out was discouraging. I just didn't want to give up without giving my best. It's hard to put your best foot forward when you aren't sure what the outcome will be. Still, we must remember that we reap what we sow even in difficult times.

When was the last time you sacrificed something you wanted for something you needed?

What motivated you to make the sacrifice?

What are some areas where you wish you had the discipline to make a change in your life?

What's keeping you from making this change?

God, help me to surrender fully to Your will. I want to give myself away to be used for Your purpose. I need Your hand on my life. Help me to see that You have greater things in store for me than even I can imagine. Amen.

19

Those Who Love You
Will Protect You

*When you value someone, you're careful how you
handle, protect, and cover them.*

So Ruth lay at Boaz's feet until the morning, but she got
up before it was light enough for people to recognize
each other. For Boaz had said, "No one must know that a
woman was here at the threshing floor."

Ruth 3:14 NLT

Before little girls turn into adult women, we are taught to approach one particular type of man with great caution. My father warned me. My mother warned me. My brothers and older girlfriends warned me. Beware of the man who considers you a conquest and brags to all of his friends about adding you to his list. Even men who don't seem to be players can sometimes betray your reputation by disregarding how things appear to other people. This kind of man cares more about his ego than about your integrity and ignores his responsibility to shelter your heart.

On the other hand, someone who truly cares for you is always thinking about your best interests. After their divinely appointed rendezvous, Boaz told Ruth that no one must know she was there with him that night. He is fully aware of the implications that could arise from their late-night meeting. Even though he knew nothing immoral or inappropriate happened, he was savvy enough to know what it might look like to others.

Boaz protected Ruth's image. Even in his excitement about their possible future, Boaz had enough foresight to look ahead and protect her from any potential disgrace. After all, Ruth had worked very hard to build a reputable name in her new home. Despite the initial rumors, she was well respected in the town because of her faithfulness to Naomi and her dedicated work ethic.

Also, keep in mind that Boaz knew he might not be able to marry Ruth. Another relative had first right of refusal according to the legal and religious customs of their culture. She might very well end up becoming betrothed to this other man, and Boaz would never have another private conversation with her. Nevertheless, he cared about protecting Ruth's integrity and reputation in the community. He was just that kind of man—someone ultimately with just as much strength of character and moral stature. He cared more about doing the right thing, and doing it to protect another person's character, than about his own gain or exploitation.

There's something to be said about someone who doesn't just understand you but also protects your worth. Those who love you don't just see you as an opportunity; they see you as a gift. When you value someone, you're careful how you handle, protect, and cover them. This is the kind of selfless, Christlike love we see described in the famous love passage of 1 Corinthians 13: "Love is patient, love is kind. It does not envy, it does not boast, it is not proud. It does not dishonor others, it is not self-seeking, it is not easily angered, it keeps no record of wrongs. Love does not delight in evil but rejoices with the truth. It always protects, always trusts, always hopes, always perseveres" (1 Corinthians 13:4–7 NIV). Is there any better description of the dedication we see in Ruth's story? It reflects both the way that she commits to Naomi and the way Boaz gives shelter to Ruth's heart.

Boaz had spent the evening with one of Bethlehem's most intriguing women, yet he still desired to protect what they shared. As a man of character, he cared more about the long-term view—their future together—than just the present moment. As the sun began to shed light on the mysteries of the evening, Boaz made sure their secret would remain safe. Perhaps he knew that premature exposure could ruin their budding relationship. Or maybe he simply wanted to make sure Ruth knew that he had her best interests at heart, that he really was a man of integrity.

Maybe you've struggled to find the same kind of man who can handle you with a selfless love as motivation. Maybe you've been afraid that such a man doesn't exist, or doesn't exist for you. It may take time, but wait for the Boaz in your life before you reveal the tenderness of your heart. If you aren't careful, you'll give yourself to someone who shares your most vulnerable moments with the world. You are far too valuable to give yourself away for bragging rights. Those who really love you will protect you from the prying eyes of the world.

Before you give your heart away, pay attention to the way those who say they love you protect your best interests. Are they concerned that others think the best of you? Do they encourage you to be your true self, your best, most authentic self? Or are they looking for subtle—or not so subtle—ways to use you for their own selfish pleasure or advancement?

You may need to make some changes or have an honest conversation with some of the people closest to you. Don't be afraid to stick up for your true worth. Those who know and genuinely love you will not perceive you as defensive, insecure, or arrogant. They will know that you only want the truth.

Journal

The hardest lesson in love I've learned at this point in my life is that love requires growth, and growth doesn't always feel good. We often confuse the type of pain that love is supposed to carry and swear off love altogether—or worse, settle. Boaz's coverage of Ruth is one of the lessons on love I cherish the most. I, like most women, long to have a husband who loves me with as much reverence. Someone who thinks beyond the moment and plans for a secure future.

Sure, there may be unforeseen circumstances that make the future difficult, but at heart we all want to be loved by someone who challenges us to be better and protects our best. That desire is what truly made me take a deeper look into the love I was accepting for myself. If that was what I truly wanted, why wasn't it what I had? When did I stop believing that I deserved to be protected?

For me, I couldn't just blame it on my ex-husband; I knew he was but a symptom. While symptoms can sometimes be as lethal as the disease, I wanted to get to the root of the problem. I believe it rested in my insecurity. I needed him to be the Band-Aid over my gunshot wound. In the end, he became a part of the infection that threatened to eat away at my hope. But the more I began to love myself, the more I realized that love can be challenging. But not just because of infidelities, finances, and other flesh issues. We have to be willing to admit that we desire protection and be vulnerable enough to trust it when it arrives.

Do you have someone in your life who can help make you think outside of the box?

How well do you receive input from your loved ones? Do you question their motives or know they have your best interests at heart?

Before Ruth could even open her mouth to consider what others would think of her late departure, Boaz was covering her. He was a few steps ahead of her. Do you have people in your life who are a few steps ahead of you?

How can you begin to invest wisdom and love into your relationships so that you are covering them?

Prayer

I need to have more wisdom in my life, God. I have no time for the distractions of trivial things; I'm preparing for my destiny. Lord, give me the spirit of discernment so I can remove anything or anyone distracting me from my destiny. Cover me with the gift of Your wisdom. Amen.

20

Relationships Are Investments

"The worst regret we have in life, is not for the wrong things we did, but for the thousands of right things we did, for the wrong people."

—*Unknown*

---

lso he said, "Bring the shawl that is on you and hold it." And when she held it, he measured six ephahs of barley, and laid it on her. Then she went into the city.

When she came to her mother-in-law, she said, "Is that you, my daughter?" Then she told her all that the man had done for her.

Ruth 3:15–16 NKJV

During my sophomore year of college, I had a schedule that gave me a lot of extra time off. Enough time, in fact, that I decided to get a part-time job. After searching the online student community for leads, I finally found a job that would allow me to tutor middle-school-aged children in the afternoons.

To say the least, I was excited. It wasn't that it was my first job. Growing up in church, I was used to working with kids all the time. Actually, it's more accurate to say that in church I was always volunteering, because the pay was love and hugs. So now I would actually have a paying job!

Because of my start date, I was told I would have to wait three weeks for my first paycheck. That was fine with me, though; a three-week wait was better than no paycheck at all. Around midnight the day of my scheduled direct deposit, I refreshed my computer screen dozens of times. There it was—all $304.87 of my first paycheck!

I was brimming with excitement! I was so proud of my first check and so excited about my first real paying job that I wanted to go celebrate. So I planned dinner with some of my friends at one of our favorite restaurants. Scheduled a nail appointment. Ran to the mall. And still had time to stop by Target to grab a couple of movies just in case the girls stayed the night.

You guessed it: I got paid Friday and my money was gone by Sunday. I learned very quickly that if I didn't start spending my money wisely, I would have nothing to show for it. As I came into adulthood, I learned the power of investing.

In its simplest form, when you invest something, whether it's your time or finances, you do so expecting a return. That's why we *spend* time and *spend* money. We give something away in hopes that what we receive back is greater than what we put in. Investing requires discipline and wisdom, an ability to plan ahead and the willpower to stick to a budget in order to sustain the plan and reap the dividends.

For a businessman like Boaz, giving away six measures of barley to Ruth was an investment. Though she had made herself available to him, he insisted on following the protocol of the land and seeking the relative that had the first right to marry her. While there were no strings attached to his gift of grain, Boaz hoped that he was creating an investment in his future with Ruth. He wanted her to know he was serious about wanting to marry her.

And even if his generous gift of grain wasn't very romantic, it still demonstrated his attitude toward her. He might not have ever benefited directly and personally from his gift, but he knew that Ruth was the kind of person worthy of it. Whether he enjoyed the dividend or Naomi or others did, Boaz knew his investment would not be wasted. He felt confident that Ruth understood what was being entrusted to her.

God invests in us the same way. Each day we're here on earth is God-given time, a divine investment. We have an opportunity to honor His investment with our mind, gifts, service, and spirit. My prayer is that we find the courage to fight whatever blocks our efforts to give God the maximum return on His investment. No matter what your challenges might be, remember that if God is still investing air into your lungs, then He still has a destiny for you.

Sometimes we assume that God's gifts to us have strings attached or the kind of fine print that we might associate with hidden fees in a bad contract. We mistakenly believe that if we fully embrace all that God has given us, He will expect us to become missionaries in some foreign country or serve in some sacrificial capacity that drains us. While we can count on being stretched, we must also remember that God has invested gifts, talents, desires, and dreams in us for a reason.

He didn't instill a dream of becoming an entrepreneur and a gift for business in someone expecting that they should preach or lead the choir. He doesn't plant seeds of creativity and artistic ability in someone so that they can become an accountant. There's nothing wrong with any of these endeavors, of course, but when we're not living out of our true gifting, we feel like the proverbial square peg trying to fit in a round hole.

Your Father knows who you are in your heart of hearts—after all, He created you this way. His investment in you is no mistake, nor is the dividend He expects going to require you to compromise your calling. When you collide with destiny as Ruth did, you will discover a beautiful point of intersection between the longings of your heart, your experience and gifting, and the opportunities God opens before you.

God wastes nothing, so use what He has given you as fuel for your soul's journey.

Many people have suggested that we can determine our true priorities by reviewing where we spend our time, our money, and our energy. Often the dissonance between what we want our priorities to be and the way we're actually living becomes too heavy to bear. We realize that something has to change. Our beliefs and values have to be tested and refined and our commitment to them exercised. If we say one thing and do another, we will naturally be unsatisfied and unhappy.

Ruth made choices that seemed risky, illogical, or even crazy at the time. But she maintained her integrity, followed her heart, and trusted God's guidance each step of the way. She refused to do what convention, tradition, or others' expectations dictated. Her courage, strength, and perseverance allowed her to blaze her own trail and establish a life that was truly unlike anyone else's. As a result, she experienced the fullness of being God's masterpiece, not a paint-by-numbers imitation of anyone else's vision.

Where do you invest the majority of your time and finances?

What do your investments say about you?

What have others invested in you?

How do you remain patient to wait on the return of your investment?

God, I know You have placed so much inside of me. Please help me see that there is life after my pain. I want to believe that I can still give You a return on Your investment. I just need the strength to move past this moment so I can live again. Amen.

21

Wait Patiently

When you're right on the edge of a breakthrough,
expect your patience to be tested.

Then she told her everything Boaz had done for her and added, "He gave me these six measures of barley, saying, 'Don't go back to your mother-in-law empty-handed.'"

Then Naomi said, "Wait, my daughter, until you find out what happens. For the man will not rest until the matter is settled today."

Ruth 3:16–18

No one informed me that buying a house is like playing "Hurry Up and Wait." Yes, it's a real game. It's the same game some hair stylists play, as well as doctors and dentists. They tell you to be on time or they'll cancel your appointment. So you arrive on time and then have to sit and wait thirty minutes at least. Complaining doesn't help—they will smile at you and act like they believe that your time is just as valuable as theirs, but nothing will change the next time. Apparently, it's just part of the hidden cost for these services.

Had I known this game is at the essence of becoming a home-owner, I would have been better prepared. But I didn't, so I emailed my lender every other day to check the status of my loan. And every other day I received the same answer: "It could be any day now, so just be patient." Hurry up and wait.

The mortgage company didn't understand. I had Pinterest boards full of my favorite designs. I'd found the perfect bed for the master bedroom, and the bed I wanted for my son, Malachi, had just gone on sale. I was excited to start nesting, but the process of waiting had become so nerve-racking.

After almost a month, I received the preapproval for my loan and put a home under contract. Then another two months went by, and I still had no status update on my final loan and when we'd close. I was within reach of my goals, so close I could brush it with my fingertips, but not there yet. I was tired of waiting and waiting, fearing something might go wrong but having no recourse except . . . to wait some more.

This in-between time when you're almost-but-not-yet can be the most frustrating time of any process. It's the moment when you can see your goal in front of you but just aren't where you want to be yet. It's the time an expectant mother feels like she can't bear to wait any longer but then realizes she still has weeks and weeks to wait. It's the season when you're waiting for your supervisor to post the new job listing, the one that matches perfectly what you've already been doing but pays significantly more. It's the unbearable "give me some space" time that a certain special someone requests as they think through whether to take your relationship to the next level. So much is about to happen no matter what happens!

In these times, patience feels like having to wear a heavy wool sweater on an unseasonably warm spring day. The sweater made sense that morning with the chill in the air, which will likely return when the sun goes down. But in the meantime, the sun has burned through the foggy haze and raised the temperature significantly. You can't take off your sweater yet, but it's driving you crazy. So you just have to bear it and look forward to the time when you walk through the door at home and can slide into sweats and a T-shirt.

Patience requires the discomfort of residing in the present even as we glimpse what's ahead. This is when we must remember that Ruth 3:18 sounds a lot like Philippians 1:6: "Being confident of this, that he who began a good work in you will carry it on to completion until the day of Christ Jesus." God will not give up on you. In church we say, "I don't believe He's brought me this far to leave me."

These are the moments when our faith becomes the only thing we have to hold on to. You did the best you could with what you were given. God blessed your work to go to the next level, and now you must see if there is even more than you dreamed of waiting for you. Ruth set out on a journey of survival and collided with her destiny. She didn't begin the process hoping to be married to the man who owned the field. She worked to better herself, and through this effort she was blessed and able to bless others.

Can you be patient while He does His good work in you?

With my home loan, I turned in all the paper work, answered every question, and faxed every document. I lined up a moving company, ordered appliances, and picked out furniture. I diligently answered every question and followed through on each form and document. There was nothing else I could do but leave it in God's hands.

When you've done all you can do, rest your mind and be at peace. You've sown all the right seeds. You've tried to right as many wrongs as you can. You continue being the best wife you can be, the best mother you can be, the best friend. Now it's time for God to do the rest. Don't give up because your harvest hasn't come quickly. The most rewarding investments take time to grow.

Journal

After I started writing the above entry, almost two more months passed before I found out I'd been approved for my final home loan. In hindsight, it doesn't really seem like the wait was that long, but maybe it's because the promise was worth it. We've already created memories, and the walls echo with our laughter.

Time is a funny thing; when you watch the clock, it never moves. When I find myself worrying about another area of my life in limbo, I try to remember that whatever the outcome is, I'll be okay. I'm still learning each day, but each time I reflect on past worries ize I survived. Our worry insults God. Our faith insists on patience, a compliment to our Creator's sovereignty.

How have you made peace with what hurt you?

What was your role in the hurt? How has your role now changed?

Did you seek forgiveness from yourself or others for your part?

Have you done all that you can do?

God, help me to humble myself to take a look on the inside. A large part of me was taken, broken from me by life. I don't want to lose anything else unless it goes to You. Your will be done, not mine. Give me the patience to wait on Your blessing. I'm ready to be restored and find the peace in my collision. Amen.

22

God Will Put Like-Minded People in Your Life

You don't have to chase people down or convince them to be in your life. God will bring the right people at the perfect time.

Meanwhile Boaz went up to the town gate and sat down there just as the guardian-redeemer he had mentioned came along. Boaz said, "Come over here, my friend, and sit down." So he went over and sat down.

Boaz took ten of the elders of the town and said, "Sit here," and they did so. Then he said to the guardian-redeemer, "Naomi, who has come back from Moab, is selling the piece of land that belonged to our relative Elimelek. I thought I should bring the matter to your attention and suggest that you buy it in the presence of these seated here and in the presence of the elders of my people. If you will redeem it, do so. But if you will not, tell me, so I will know. For no one has the right to do it except you, and I am next in line."

"I will redeem it," he said.

Ruth 4:1-4

t's been bittersweet to see how some of my friendships have changed over time. And it's been especially surprising to see the way friends' lives and lifestyles change as well. Everyone grows at a different rate. Often when we change for the better, we want people in our lives who are like-minded so that we can be motivated to stay the course.

These might not be the same people who were part of your earlier journey. Part of growing and changing means knowing which relationships to maintain and which ones to recognize as only for a season. Just because you've been friends with someone for years doesn't mean that they are maturing at the same speed or even in the same direction that you're traveling. It's not easy, but sometimes you have to consider leaving some people behind as they venture in directions that are not your own.

Had you asked Ruth about her BFF back in Moab, she might have said it was her sister-in-law Orpah. We can't know this for sure, but it seems plausible. After all, they married into the same family, they came from the same land, and they spent plenty of time with each other. The fact that both younger women initially left with Naomi indicates that they both shared some similar values as well as an affection for their mother-in-law.

When Orpah decided to stay in Moab, Ruth chose not to stay with her. Had Ruth stayed there, she never would have learned what she was really made of. Perhaps she would have married again, and maybe her friendship with her sister-in-law would have endured. But in pursuit of her divine destiny, Ruth had to take a risk. Staying was fine for Orpah, but Ruth wanted more. There comes a time in life when we are ready to go to the next level. We must embrace the reality that everyone cannot go with us.

Orpah and Ruth did not have to quarrel to separate. They simply understood that their destinies were no longer tied to each other. So often we decide we will pursue our dream if someone else lands their dream job. Or we'll wait to go back to school until our friends also have the money to enroll. We don't want to better ourselves until others can handle the better us.

You cannot let your life be dictated by the reaction of others, though. Ultimately God has preordained your future, and He doesn't need the lives of your friends to parallel everything He has planned for you. Don't handcuff someone to your dream. They don't have to believe with you or cheer for you if God is with you. It may be lonely at times, but He will provide the right relationships at the right time. Don't be afraid to release old friendships into God's hands in order to follow the calling He has placed on your life.

Making the decision to divorce was one of the most difficult yet necessary things I've ever had to do. I wanted so badly to have a husband to love me that I married the first man who said, "I love you and I don't want anything from you." The problem was that I wanted so much from him. I wanted him to become someone he'd never shown any signs of being. I chased him down to be in my life; when I finally got him, I wanted him to change who he was.

I had a laundry list of things he needed to change—no more infidelity, more responsibility with our finances, more involvement with the children—before my picture could be perfect. We were two selfish people fighting for the right to be selfish and loved unconditionally at the same time. When I started loving myself by experiencing God's love, I realized that marriage was so much more than finding someone to make you feel better about yourself.

My journey of loving me required that I correct a lot of wrongs I'd done in the name of my insecurity. I had to mend some relationships and let others go. Above all, I had to be at peace with myself. I had to be comfortable being alone, but not lonely. I had to free my ex-husband to be with someone who loved him for him and not for what they were trying to heal in him, and I deserved the same.

You may have to spend some time alone while you find your way, but there are lessons in that, too. Ruth strived to live a life of integrity and commitment. She did what was right even if it meant it would hurt. Whether gleaning the leftovers in the field or consoling a bitter Naomi during her most difficult days, Ruth proved she was dedicated to the process.

Boaz knew he didn't have the first claim to marry Ruth, so he followed the protocol. How fitting that without her even realizing it, God had brought someone into her life who had the same level of commitment to integrity. By the time Boaz approached the other kinsman, Boaz had already shown interest in Ruth. He had invested in her and had firsthand knowledge of her virtue. But he knew he had to do the right thing even at the risk of losing her.

You don't have to chase people down or convince them to be in your life. God will bring the right people at the perfect time. Don't spend a lifetime holding yourself back because others do not want to go with you. If it comes down to following them or pursuing your destiny, make the right decision.

Journal

It's good to have friends along the route of our destiny, but sometimes we may not even know the people who inspire us to greatness.

Ruth's story remains relevant and resonant to us today because of her character, her actions, and her faith. Other people throughout history can also ignite our imaginations and motivate us to fulfill our destiny. We see how they handled adversity and realize that we are not alone, even if no one is literally beside us.

I have packed a lot of living into my relatively short life. So I wanted to share what I have learned so far, which I've done in my memoir, *Lost and Found*. I'm far from having all the answers, but I do know what it means to overcome setbacks and less-than-satisfactory situations in order to discover what God has for me. In my teen years, I never would have dreamed of doing what I'm doing now. But I've been blessed with people in my life who have reinforced the fulfillment of my becoming the woman God made me to be. I pray the same for you on your journey!

Do you have someone in your life who's just as focused and driven as you are? How have you been motivated by their ambition?

Are there others you've been waiting on instead of moving forward on your own path? How have they slowed down your progress?

Ask God to bring people who can help you maximize your potential.

How do you bring out the best in the people in your life?

Prayer

God, thank You for the times of isolation. These times alone have helped me to realize the hunger inside of me. I pray that when the time is right You will bring into my life people who understand that I am destiny-focused. I'm thankful for Your perfect timing in my life, and for the people You place in my life according to Your infinite wisdom. Amen.

23

Set Your Standards

We all must set our price, and it can't fluctuate depending on who's interested. Your price is your price. Those who want to be in your life can afford to invest or they can't.

Then Boaz told him, "Of course, your purchase of the land from Naomi also requires that you marry Ruth, the Moabite widow. That way she can have children who will carry on her husband's name and keep the land in the family."

Ruth 4:5 NLT

One of my favorite parts of vacationing at the beach is shopping. I don't mean going to a mall, either. I mean sitting on golden sands haggling underneath the warm sun with local vendors at open-air stalls. Often I don't even have to go looking for them—they come to me. From fresh fruit to sunglasses, wristwatches to home decor, almost everything comes along if you stay in one spot. What makes it the most fun is talking someone out of their price. I always feel like I've gotten a bargain by playing the game.

I've noticed these tropical entrepreneurs always manage to bring the price down once you seem to lose interest. Desperate for the sale, they start throwing in things for free or slashing the price in half. They will do whatever it takes to close the deal. And I'm not the only tourist who enjoys this unique kind of retail adventure. At the end of the day, my family and friends all gather for dinner and talk about the deals we made while relaxing on the beach.

Unfortunately, sometimes we conduct our relationships as if we are selling souvenirs on the seashore. We haggle, we negotiate, we compromise—too fearful of being alone to stand firm on the value of our true worth. Why do we insist on giving ourselves away? Offering up piece after piece of ourselves so that someone gets us at a steal? I don't know about you, but I want to be valued. If you don't see yourself as a gift, then who will? We must set our standards and hold firm on our price. It's better to walk away than to lower our self-worth to less than its actual value.

From the very beginning of their meeting, Boaz informed his kinsman of the terms. Along with Ruth, he would be responsible for having a child—heirs were vital to the family lineage—and caring for Naomi. Boaz knew that she was a widow from Moab as well as a noble woman of amazing strength. He recognized that someone else had a claim to her first, and he did the right thing by allowing this relative the opportunity his status afforded. But when given the opportunity himself, Boaz was more than willing to commit to paying full price. These were the expectations that came with the responsibility. There was no sticker shock for Boaz; he knew the price and was gladly willing to pay it.

What are your expectations, your standards? In other words, what's your price?

Have you shared those expectations with others? We get upset when people do not live up to the standards we set, but often we have not even given them the courtesy of letting them know these standards exist.

Likewise, we cannot get caught up trying to meet the standards of others and fail to birth the vision God has for us. I'm here to let you know that God has placed talents and gifts inside of us— and He has plans for us to make the best use of those talents and gifts. Our faith teaches us that taking a stand to reach our goals may have a cost. People laughed at Noah and looked at David in shock. Those called by God must be willing to have faith strong enough to withstand the rejection of others around them.

There are some things in life that should be nonnegotiable. Your character, your self-esteem, your ambition are the things that make you, *you*! If someone wants to be in your life, you owe it to them to let them know up front what you will and will not compromise on.

And if you have not considered the boundaries of your own worth, then others will attempt to lower them for you. Some people do this to feel better about themselves; others do it because they want to control you or manipulate circumstances. Regardless of how it happens, the place to begin defending against this kind of price reduction is within. No one can force you to sell yourself short if you're aware of your true worth.

God loves you enough to rescue you, redeem you, and elevate you to new levels of stewardship. He knows what you've been through, how you've failed, and what your heart hopes. And His price has remained the same from the day you were born: He loved you enough to send His Son to die for you. God loves you enough to pursue you even when you've tried to push Him away. He knows you are His precious child and wants you to know it as well.

We all must set our price, and it can't fluctuate depending on who's interested. Your price is your price. Those who want to be in your life can afford to rise to the occasion. Don't give yourself away to the lowest bidder because you're afraid no one else will want you.

Journal

Sometimes when you love someone, you become willing to change in order to show that person that love. While every relationship requires some give-and-take, there should be boundaries that cannot be crossed. Some are obvious, such as physical abuse and domestic violence. Others may be more subtle, such as emotional abuse or controlling behavior. As we see with Boaz and Ruth, a relationship built on love for each other and faith in God forms a gold-standard, blue-chip investment.

The same is true for relationships in our families. My sister and I are complete opposites in many ways but just alike in others. As we came into adulthood, we began to explore those differences independently. We had to take on the responsibility of learning how to love one another when we were no longer sharing a room.

When we were both in college with our own sets of friends, we had to learn to share one another and still trust our bond was strong. I learned that I couldn't just depend on history to protect our future. If I wanted to remain close, it would take effort. We've learned to balance one another's personalities and social circles. There are some people I will have to be close to because I'm loyal to my sister. There will be times when she has to understand that my friends could never replace her role. It is important that we don't ask others around us to give more than we are willing to return.

List five nonnegotiable standards you have for your relationships.

Why are they so important to you?

Have you lived up to the same standards in return consistently, never ceasing? Have you been forgiving when others fall short?

Have you prayed over your standards?

God, help me to become a better version of me. I no longer want to bend my standards to accommodate another's insecurity. Lord, help me to walk boldly and proudly into my next level. As You develop me into a better person, I pray You will help me to eliminate anything that removes the ultimate standard: Your promise on my life. Amen.

24

Be Honest

So often we take on person after person, struggle after struggle, only to find ourselves completely depleted. We must know our limits if we are to remain on the path to our divine destiny.

The closest relative said, "I cannot redeem it for myself, because I would jeopardize my own inheritance. Redeem it for yourself; you may have my right of redemption, for I cannot redeem it."

Ruth 4:6 NASB

used to envy those people who could say no. Especially the ones who made it look natural and even kind, not harsh or defensive. It's not that I couldn't say it, but I didn't like to hurt people's feelings. It seemed like the more I didn't want to do something, the worse it became. I felt bad about agreeing to do something I didn't want to do, and even worse about not being able to say no.

Then I became one of those people.

I started to reason with myself. Is it better to disappoint someone up front or to start something knowing that I can't give 100 percent? I battled with this for so long before I realized that at the end of the day, I was doing them, and myself, a major disservice. I was spreading myself too thin trying to be what everyone needed me to be. Learning to stand up for my peace has been a process, because I want so badly to help others have their peace. I'm learning that there are only a few people who should have access to disturb my atmosphere.

We often find ourselves completely stressed over things and people we may only briefly encounter. Ultimately, we have to preserve our energy for our own missions of service. When we help others, we must do so at the urging of God, not for their approval.

How often do we allow our hearts to commit to something we physically, emotionally, or mentally can't continue? So often we take on person after person, struggle after struggle, only to find ourselves completely depleted and unable to follow through. So often we see people who stop what they're doing to start something else. They become a jack- or jill-of-all-trades and master of none.

And if our own personality and inner perfectionist weren't enough, our culture constantly encourages us to do more, be more, juggle more, and balance more without recognizing that we all have limitations. Our bodies need rest and sleep just as our hearts need time to consider what we prize the most.

When Boaz approached the other kinsman, certainly this man had heard of Ruth. He undoubtedly knew her story and the tales that were told of her loyalty. Yet this kinsman still decided his inheritance was more important than the opportunity.

I have met countless people whom I feel I could be great friends with, but I really don't have time to invest in every one of these opportunities. It doesn't make the people bad or unworthy. It simply means I have to save a piece of myself, for myself, as well as for the others to whom I've already committed.

Social media allows us to connect with one another quickly and conveniently, but even with the advantages of technology, we have to be careful that we're not distracting ourselves from investing in actual relationships. We have to know our priorities and make them paramount in the choices we make each day.

We don't have to create some huge profound reason for why we can't do something. We can simply say no and have peace about it.

For this other kinsman, it was as simple as, "I'm pursuing my inheritance and can't be distracted." He knew that if he married a Moabite woman, he would jeopardize his family inheritance. It was the price he would have to pay, and for him it was too high. He may not have realized what he was passing up, but in one sense it didn't matter because he was already committed to maintaining certain priorities. His decision cannot be deemed as either right or wrong but simply what was best for him at that time. Ultimately, the kinsman did everyone a favor. By being honest, he did not hinder Boaz or Ruth—or himself—from receiving God's best for their lives.

As you continue on your journey, you do not have to be connected with everyone you encounter. There are many people who will never be tied to your destiny, no more than this kinsman was tied to Ruth's. Be realistic about what you can and cannot handle. Do not let the fear of disappointing someone cause you to disturb God's master plan. Once you determine your purpose, stick to it and don't let anything distract you from staying the course.

It takes a person of strong character to be able to say no. When Naomi told Ruth to return to Moab, it was an opportunity to take an easy out and go back home. But Ruth knew where her heart was leading her, and therefore she refused. This other kinsman also knew where his own destiny was leading, and it was not with Ruth. As long as we're committed to living from our hearts and not just our heads, from our faith and not just our fantasies, then we will find the power to say no when we need it. No shame, no regret, no recrimination.

Journal

I know what it's like to be a "people pleaser." When I first entered college, I majored in business with the intent of becoming an accountant. It wasn't that I loved numbers and accounting so much as it was a personal motivation. After giving birth to my son at such a young age, I wanted to do something that would prove my worth to my parents, especially my father. So I thought that if I became an accountant and worked for the church, then he would be proud of me.

It was a long time before I realized that I wasn't created or called to be an accountant, and a little while longer yet before I could share this with my dad. What I learned, of course, is that he and my mom are proud of me and love me just for who I am. I didn't have to try to make up for the past or prove myself professionally. If I had been honest with myself from the start, I could have bypassed that little detour. Nonetheless, God has used it to lead me on the path where I find myself now. That's the beauty of redemption and restoration—He uses what we give Him to create something divine.

Do you ever worry about letting people down?

Are you losing yourself trying to help or befriend others?

How can you begin to eliminate the responsibilities and relationships that are weighing you down?

Each little piece of you counts. Make a list and prioritize what is most important in your life.

God, help me to be honest about my limitations. Help me to realize when some need me but when others need You. I don't want to be so wrapped up helping others that I cease to pursue my destiny. I pray that You give others the help they need to find their peace. Please give me the wisdom not to let people interrupt my peace or rob me of my ambition. Amen.

25

It's Already Done

When you are walking in obedience, you have to believe God is going to cover you.

Now in those days it was the custom in Israel for anyone transferring a right of purchase to remove his sandal and hand it to the other party. This publicly validated the transaction. So the other family redeemer drew off his sandal as he said to Boaz, "You buy the land."

Ruth 4:7–8 NLT

Waiting on a decision that will have an impact on your future is never easy. Whether it's waiting to hear test results from your doctor, watching for an email with the response to your application, or counting the days until you receive someone else's response to your invitation, the suspense kills you. Your mind tries to think through all the variations of what could happen, might happen, will happen. You imagine the best case, the worst case, and all the possibilities in between. Clearly, something is about to happen that will alter the path you are on, but you can't yet determine which way the road sign will point.

Boaz had explained the situation to the kinsman who had first rights to marry Ruth and continue the family legacy. He did the honorable thing by playing fair and going directly to the man and explaining the situation. But clearly, after the night when Ruth sneaked into his threshing room, Boaz hoped that somehow this unique and beautiful woman would be his wife. Like an attorney making his closing argument, he would now have to wait to see what the other man would decide.

Somewhere on the other side of town, Ruth and Naomi were waiting anxiously to hear which kinsman redeemer would take Ruth as his wife. They had no clue that they were anxious for no reason. Long before Ruth met Boaz or even her first husband,

Mahlon, God had predestined her steps. She was on reserve for her divine destiny.

How befitting it is that the kinsman takes off his shoe and gives it to Boaz. In their time, removing a sandal and handing it over was to say, "My feet will not walk on your ground." Or perhaps another way of saying this would be, "I don't want to step on your toes. Here, you go ahead." With this simple act, Ruth had officially become Boaz's betrothed, even if she wasn't aware of it yet. She may have felt nervous, but had nothing to worry about.

Can you relate? Anyone who's been through what you've been through would have lost his or her mind by now. One thing after another, tears after tears, yet you are still here. You're tired, you're weary, and you're still harboring old fears of what could go wrong. But now is the time to keep your faith firmly rooted in the goodness of your loving Father's character. He has been strengthening you, refining you, building you up to handle what lies ahead. You may feel like it's taking too long, or even that the Lord has forgotten you. But consider this: Could it be that God has you on reserve? You may not realize it, but you were bought with a cost. You have been placed on reserve for a higher purpose.

That's why that accident couldn't kill you or the disease missed you. You didn't finish your degree the first time so that you would have the experience to land the promotion you wanted. You handled it all as best you could. Through breakups and makeups, you were placed on reserve. The incidents of the past were stepping-stones to reach the other side of the shore, where your feet are about to walk.

Ruth's situation reminds me of another passage that should give us confidence. Theologians believe that Genesis 3:15 is a prophecy of the coming of Christ: "And I will put enmity between you and the woman, and between your seed and her Seed; he shall bruise your head, and you shall bruise His heel" (NKJV). Here, after all that business with forbidden fruit, God tells Satan that the woman's offspring, humans, will always war against him. In fact,

God promises that Eve's descendants will wound Satan's head, while he will only wound their heels. The enemy may have won a temporary battle of temptation, but he would lose the final war.

It seems a bit unfair. A head wound is almost always more dangerous than a wound to the heel. Unless, of course, that heel wound makes you take a few missteps. When our heels have been bruised, we start to walk on land that we shouldn't. We begin to be poisoned by our own fear, bitterness, anger, and doubt. We cannot let what happened to us then consume us now. We may have a limp, but the enemy will ultimately be crushed as we persevere in the power of the Lord.

Through Christ we are able to recover from the bruises of life that can lead us astray. Certainly Ruth knew all too well about the detours of life. As she waited for new information on where her journey would lead her, she had no idea God had already marked her path.

We often worry ourselves sick about something God has already figured out. When you are walking in obedience, you have to believe God is going to cover you. Whether things go the way you think they should or not, when you're walking with Him, you can trust that He will transform every trial.

Don't be tricked into thinking that just because you're delayed you're also denied. Stay the course, heal your heel, regain your footing, and prepare to use your destiny to wound the enemy's head.

My son is in the fifth grade. Almost every evening we have the same routine, but it took us about two and a half months of the school year to get one. Before then I started realizing why my mother always told us that the infant stage is one of the easier parts of parenting.

My little boy is approaching teenhood, with all of the melodrama that comes with it. During those first few months of fifth grade, the recaps of his day's events read like a script from the Disney show *Recess*. His schoolwork was missing and grades were beginning to slip. I wasn't impressed. I didn't want him to be tempted to use the "mean teacher" excuse. I wanted him to know that we could face whatever he was up against at school, but I needed him to do his part: turn in his homework, remember his planner, pay attention in class, and more.

I promised that if he did his part, then I would defend him if necessary to his teachers. We often want God to defend us, but we don't do our part. If we believe that our fate lies in His hands, then our responsibility is to give each assignment our best effort. We have to trust that our Father will do everything we need in order to succeed.

In what areas of your life are you waiting on God to move?

Have you committed those areas to prayer, or have you given up?

How can you exercise more faith and effort in the pursuit of your purpose?

What will you do once you've received your breakthrough? How will your life be different as you collide with your destiny?

God, I ask that You give me the patience to deal with silence. Help me to see that my faith must be proven, tested, and then stretched. I know that being a Christian is more than just quoting Scriptures and going to church. I believe in Your Word and trust that everything will work out for me. Even when You are silent, I trust that You still hear my prayers and see my faith. Amen.

26

"I Know You, and I Still Chose You"

We often allow the things that almost broke us to define us and keep us from reaching the next level.

Then Boaz announced to the elders and all the people, "Today you are witnesses that I have bought from Naomi all the property of Elimelek, Kilion and Mahlon. I have also acquired Ruth the Moabite, Mahlon's widow, as my wife, in order to maintain the name of the dead with his property, so that his name will not disappear from among his family or from his hometown. Today you are witnesses!"

Ruth 4:9–10

When my sister and I were growing up, we fell in love with the movie *Pretty Woman*. It's the story of a young woman, living a less than desirable lifestyle, and a wealthy man who offers to pay her to accompany him to high-society events. In one scene, Vivian, the lead character played by Julia Roberts, walks into a fancy store on Rodeo Drive and is rudely ignored.

It's not that the sales staff don't see her; they just don't like what they see. She is underdressed and doesn't appear to have the income necessary to shop at their store. They were right about her and wrong about her at the same time. They could not distinguish her current state from the promise residing in her future.

She returns to the hotel embarrassed and upset because they confirmed what she has felt all along: She's not good enough. Later in the movie, after she has been expensively clothed and elegantly groomed, she returns to the same store. Instantly a snobby associate rushes to greet her. But Vivian reminds the snooty clerk of her previous visit and how she was treated. With her hands full of bags from the surrounding high-end boutiques, she tells the saleslady, "Big mistake! *Huge!*"

It's one of the most memorable moments in the movie. The core of what most people love about this part is the lesson it teaches. It's what anyone who has ever been labeled and misjudged desires others to realize. We should never judge someone before his or her transformation is complete.

Vivian was the same woman each time she entered the fancy boutique. But the sales associates only deemed her worthy when she wore expensive clothes along with the right styling and makeup. Their standard only allowed them to evaluate people based on appearance, status, and wealth. Although they probably knew that many attractive, wealthy people are not kind, compassionate, or considerate, their goal was on their own opportunity to make money.

When Vivian returned, she relished the opportunity to rub the saleswoman's mistake in her face. She got to do what we've all wanted to do at times—show people that we are worth more than the way we've been treated by them. What's the old saying, "The best revenge is living well"? The best revenge is showing others who you really are and being humble enough not to say "I told you so."

Ruth probably knew what this feeling was like. The town's most respected man had declared his desire to marry Ruth to anyone who would listen. Ruth, the same foreign woman locals once whispered about, would soon be married to the esteemed and wealthy Boaz. Had they judged her when she was on the road to Bethlehem, they also would have made a "Big mistake! Huge!"

Too often we prefer to believe the things that almost broke us will keep us from reaching the next level. Clinging to such a false belief in turn relieves us of the responsibility of persevering. We think if we define ourselves by the past, then we don't have to try moving into the future. *Wrong*. Just because you once made poor decisions doesn't mean you can't be used for a better purpose.

God has the power to change people's lives, from the inside out. Others may not be able to see all that He is accomplishing inside you. They might not yet glimpse the strength, the determination, the talent, and the dedication that God has been refining and polishing within you. Your time to shine, though, will soon allow everyone to see just what He has purposed for you.

God knows exactly who you are and the pain you've had to experience to birth your destiny. He knows everything, the good and the bad. He knows you and He still chose you. You don't have to work harder, dress differently, have a *Pretty Woman* makeover, or shop in Beverly Hills. You can come as you are, just as you are, knowing that God has seen you as the King's daughter all along.

The time will come, like it did for Boaz and Ruth, when others will witness the redemptive transformation God has been accomplishing inside you. Until then, you simply have to continue on your journey, led by God's guidance and not by what other people may think of you. The day will come when those around you realize that they were mistaken to have labeled you, dismissed you, or ignored you. They will see who you really are.

Journal

I think one of the moments of my first pregnancy that gets the most affectionate responses is my father's commitment to vouching for me. In spite of my mistakes and flaws, he stood by my side. He never made me feel like he chose the congregation over our connection.

This moment in Ruth's story is so priceless to me because we see Boaz vouching for her. And in order to vouch for her, he listed all the things that she probably thought would stop her. She was qualified, not because she did everything right, but because she handled even her wrongs with grace. Grace removes the limits that exist in our life. Often the things we spend a lifetime trying to hide are the very tools we need to become who God has called us to be. I assumed that my father wouldn't want to vouch for me because there were times I couldn't vouch for myself. I didn't realize that's what love is all about.

What's a remaining limitation on your journey to greatness?

Is it possible to use this to help you instead of letting it hold you back?

Can your story help someone else close a chapter in their life?

Name three things pain has taught you that might also serve as clues to your purpose.

Prayer

Lord, I need Your help to forgive myself. I need to rediscover my worth. Help me to see that in spite of what I have felt, I still have purpose. Release me from the shame of my past. I want to be free from the memories that haunt me so I can walk boldly on the path before me. Amen.

27

Witness the Redemption

You don't have to prove yourself to those who doubt you. When you play your part and stay the course, God will vindicate you.

All the people who were in the court, and the elders, said, "We are witnesses. May the Lord make the woman who is coming into your home like Rachel and Leah, both of whom built the house of Israel; and may you achieve wealth in Ephrathah and become famous in Bethlehem. Moreover, may your house be like the house of Perez whom Tamar bore to Judah, through the offspring which the Lord will give you by this young woman."

Ruth 4:11-12 NASB

The first time I went to see a professional basketball game, it was the Dallas Mavericks against the Los Angeles Lakers. Growing up, I had a very small, minor-stalker obsession with Kobe Bryant, but we'll save those stories for another time. So for my first game, I donned my Bryant jersey and walked proudly into the American Airlines Center with my family.

It was great—our seats were so close I could see sweat dripping off the players! As we enjoyed the intense game, I made small talk with fellow Lakers fans around me. We laughed and made playful banter with the Mavs fans throughout the evening. One gentleman in particular seemed very knowledgeable about the Lakers and clearly loved to interact with other fans.

After a hard-fought battle, the Lakers finally won the game. As we were walking out to the car, we ran into some members of our church. They had seen us during the game but couldn't get our attention. One of the deacons mentioned to me how cool it must have been to watch the Lakers game with the owner of the team. I looked over my shoulder, searching for whomever he was talking to. Then I realized he was talking to me!

I had no clue that I had been sitting beside Jerry Buss, the owner of the Lakers, the entire game. I certainly didn't ask, and he didn't mention it. We simply enjoyed watching the game together. He was down-to-earth, warm, friendly—and clearly very comfortable with himself and confident about who he was. He didn't immediately identify himself or begin name-dropping and trying to impress everyone around him. Content to be who he was, Mr. Buss made me appreciate and like him that much more.

He modeled a profound truth for me. When you are truly comfortable with who you are, you don't have to convince others of your worth. In time, others may find out, maybe they won't, but neither should determine how you live your life. Too often, we waste precious time and energy trying to live up to the standards of others while neglecting our own dreams and priorities. The one-upmanship game will always exist, and many people will probably continue to play it, whether it has to do with their clothes, house, car, education, job, or church. But along with Mr. Buss, Ruth reminds us that you don't have to be one of them.

Without trying to defend against every vicious attack or track down every person who ever said anything about her, Ruth gained the respect of everyone in Bethlehem when Boaz chose her. He stood with Ruth, and because of his position others saw her differently. Ruth didn't have to scheme for attention or revenge; she just had to go about the business of surviving.

Sometimes we're tempted to announce our redemption to validate our worth. But when you play your part and stay in position, God will vindicate you. The same mouths that once talked badly about you will be telling others they're proud of you. Be comfortable enough with who you are that you don't feel the urge to prove yourself to everyone you encounter.

There was no need for Mr. Buss to prove his worth to me at the Lakers game or for Ruth to prove her worth to the town. All she needed to do was live a life that would tell the story on its own. You don't have time to change the thoughts of everyone who ever believed differently about you. You don't have time to tell everyone your worth. Instead, let your worth do the talking.

I know this concept is always easier said than done for most of us. When I made the decision to separate in my marriage, I couldn't help but incessantly check my ex-husband's Twitter page to see what he was saying about me. I wanted to know what rumors could be created from our respective reactions. I wanted to control what could be said about me.

The more time I spent incessantly tracing down every possibility, though, the less time I had to focus on the things in my life that held the most promise. If the possibility holds no promise, it is merely a hobby. I did not want to spend time preparing for hurt. I know the rumors hurt, especially when they're so far from the truth, but the truth will always outrun the rumor mill.

Coming from a family that is often in the spotlight, I learned at an early age how frustrating and painful gossip can be, especially when it's played out on a national stage. Tabloids, TV shows, and radio programs don't always care about the truth as much as they care about stirring up controversy and creating buzz. Their primary goal is to sell their product to increase their audience so that they can charge more to advertisers.

If you try to play nice and cater to the way they do business, it will only bite you. If you ignore them, they still print or say what they want. So you have to learn to live in the tension of gossip and rumors while keeping your eyes fixed on the truth of who you are. Even when headlines cause heartaches, others will see the truth as they watch how you handle your success.

How have you handled rumors or gossip in your own life?

When you walk into a room, does your presence reflect your pain or your destiny?

You can't control what others think about you, but you do control what you project. What little changes can you begin to make that will allow others a preview of your healed future?

List those who have seen the wrong turns on your journey and yet still see your worth.

God, when You deliver me, help me to be humble enough to forgive. I want to release the anger I felt about the people who devalued me. I want to release the feelings of hurt from gossip. I know You have plans for me that are bigger and better than I can imagine. I just hope You will teach me the art of redemption. Amen.

28

From Redemption to Restoration

Restoration is one step beyond redemption. It is the moment when God shows you that you lost nothing in the process.

So Boaz took Ruth and she became his wife. When he made love to her, the Lord enabled her to conceive, and she gave birth to a son. The women said to Naomi: "Praise be to the Lord, who this day has not left you without a guardian-redeemer. May he become famous throughout Israel! He will renew your life and sustain you in your old age. For your daughter-in-law, who loves you and who is better to you than seven sons, has given him birth."

Then Naomi took the child in her arms and cared for him. The women living there said, "Naomi has a son!" And they named him Obed. He was the father of Jesse, the father of David.

Ruth 4:13–16

There are moments during pregnancy, especially for first-time mothers, when you feel like you're losing more than you're gaining. During labor pains, you don't have a concrete understanding that the increasingly painful contractions will give way to this beautiful soul you will soon hold in your arms. It's not until that instant of finally holding your newborn that you know you would do it all again, all for that timeless moment in which you are forever changed.

Many women can give birth, but it takes a mother's heart to love a child. From the time that infant is placed in her arms, she silently vows to walk through life with him or her. Her sole mission is to be the child's protector. Without even having to think about it, a mother commits to seeing problems before they happen, handling each day with care, sheltering her child.

In the same way, God is not only our Creator but also our loving Father. He created us with a purpose and loves us too much to let us go. Even when we can't understand the painful losses in our journey, we have to realize that He is working out the details of our destiny. Just as the birthing process requires pain to bring new life, we must often experience trials before we taste triumph.

Boaz helped deliver Ruth, but only God could restore her. Ruth had been content living in Moab as Mahlon's wife. But God led her and Naomi back to Bethlehem, where Boaz redeemed her from her past and then God restored all that she had lost. No longer would they face famine, for God had blessed them with one of the most abundant fields. No longer would Naomi know sadness, for God had given her a grandson to rejuvenate her joy. Ruth was no longer a widow, but rather the wife of a well-respected man. Naomi, who had lost two sons, now had the love of a daughter-in-law who had proven she was worth seven sons.

Restoration is one step past redemption. It is the moment when God shows you that you lost nothing in the process. All the tears you cried and pain you felt were a part of the plan. Anyone who has experienced the exceedingly abundant blessings of God knows that the pain pales in comparison to His restoration.

Of course, nothing can truly take the place of what you have lost. Restoration is simply a greater appreciation of God's blessings in light of knowing what you've lost. When we lose loved ones, opportunities, jobs, and relationships, we wonder if we'll ever love again, risk again, work again, or connect again. We endure loneliness and suffer from the isolation we often impose on ourselves. Then we begin to heal and experience the balm of God's presence. Eventually, we collide with our destiny and reap an abundance beyond what we lost, and often beyond what we expected.

In fact, when you give your life to God, all the seeds you sow will reap a harvest you can't even imagine. Ruth was first married to a man who left his homeland because of a famine. She went back to his land and married Boaz, the owner of one of the largest fields. She never had children with Mahlon, but with Boaz she became a mother. Ruth certainly sowed many tears, but she reaped incredible joy.

Your story is not over yet. Don't harden your heart and block the seeds from being sown. Keep your heart open and available to God. The pain may be devastating. There will be days when you want to give in and give up. You'll want to numb the pain with a masquerade, but don't. Keep walking. Keep your heart alive. And one day you'll be like Ruth, blessed by the same things that once broke you.

She didn't commit to Naomi, gather grain for their meals, or risk meeting Boaz in order to achieve financial or personal gain. The blessings simply emerged as by-products of her obedience and God's faithfulness. There's nothing wrong with wanting to be blessed, but if we put our energy into earning it, we often miss what God wants to teach us along the way.

Ruth did what she needed to do, what God led her to do, without knowing where she would end up. She didn't know how her story would end—that people thousands of years later are still reading about her, that she would become a matriarch in the lineage of God's own Son, Jesus—so she just kept allowing God to turn the next page.

Journal

The mere fact that you're reading the book of a divorced twenty-five-year-old who became a mother as a teen is incredible. I thought that my detours in life would reroute my destination completely. I wouldn't be able to accomplish some things as quickly as others because I'd been slowed down a bit.

As my friends graduated from college, I celebrated with them but secretly envied their success. I had an NFL husband, but he wasn't being faithful. It looked as though we'd all found our way. That couldn't be further from the truth for me. When I did divorce, I thought it would isolate me even more. Still, God saw my heart and blessed me in spite of my mistakes and losses. The culmination of the pain and the beauty in my life made me who I am. For so long I thought my scars made me damaged; I never realized they were the perfect canvas for grace.

Ruth recovered more than she lost. But first she had to have less than she hoped for. In what areas have you experienced having less than you hope for?

Boaz told the whole community about his love for Ruth. How is God revealing your destiny to those around you?

Who are the people God has brought into your life to share your destiny?

If you want to sow healthy seeds with your abundant blessing, you have to be willing to stretch. Are you ready to lose your control over your life and receive God's direction?

Prayer

Help me to deal with the pain of going to a new level. I want to use my blessings to help people, but I'm not sure if they'll accept me because of my past. All I desire is to help someone become free from the chains that once bound me. Give me the strength to go from redemption to restoration. Amen.

29

It's Not About You

What if your struggles are not about you but about the life that will be birthed through you?

Then Naomi took the child and laid him on her bosom, and became a nurse to him. Also the neighbor women gave him a name, saying, "There is a son born to Naomi." And they called his name Obed. He is the father of Jesse, the father of David.

Now this is the genealogy of Perez: Perez begot Hezron; Hezron begot Ram, and Ram begot Amminadab; Amminadab begot Nahshon, and Nahshon begot Salmon; Salmon begot Boaz, and Boaz begot Obed; Obed begot Jesse, and Jesse begot David.

Ruth 4:16–22 NKJV

Who would've thought that a woman who started her life worshiping idols would be part of the ancestry of Christ? Ruth gave birth to Obed, who is the father of Jesse, who is the father of David. One simple act of not falling back into the Moabite mindset after the death of Mahlon allowed her to become part of the lineage of Jesus Christ.

You may think that your survival is just for you, and that's why it's easy to let life beat you down. But it's more than that. You may not have any idea how God will use you to fulfill His divine design and to advance His kingdom. Whether you're more of a behind-the-scenes type or someone who craves the spotlight, each of us is a main character in the grand story God continues to write.

Yes, you may feel as though your life is a story unto itself, but ultimately it's one piece in the puzzle of history, one corner in the majestic mural of eternity that God is creating. Your choices matter in ways that you might never get to see while here on earth. Even decisions that may seem insignificant to you can be used by God to create a domino sequence of events.

Remember, if Ruth had not agreed to accompany Naomi back to Bethlehem, she never would have been out in the field gathering grain. If she hadn't been out there collecting leftover kernels, she would not have been noticed by Boaz. We live from day to day without being able to get a view from the heights of heaven. But Ruth's barriers became her bridges.

Christ faced His own obstacles and struggles on the road of His divinity. But He would survive and go on to fulfill His destiny, just like those who came before Him. Your commitment to surviving leaves an inheritance to your family. Only those who care to study Ruth's life understand the trouble she faced on the road to her destiny. Her story reminds us that it's not all about us. We think our survival is just for us and that's why it's tempting to stay down when we fall.

So often we remember Ruth with Boaz and her ultimate blessing, not with her struggle. This outcome gives me comfort. It means when all is said and done, my legacy will not be *what* broke me but *how* God blessed me. Only those who care to see my scars will understand that the blessing did not come without wounds and that I did all I could to survive.

Recently, I met a young lady with a beautiful, intricate tattoo woven around her left forearm. When I complimented her on it, she looked at me sheepishly and then tears began to form in her eyes. As we chatted, she went on to tell me about her struggle with cutting herself when she was a teenager. She developed numerous scars on her arm from her battles with depression and anxiety. Now, several years later, she had decided to transform the pain into a work of art, a tree of life with her scars turned into budding branches. She had literally created a reminder of how God had brought her out of her darkness and into His light.

So what story will your wounds tell? Will they be of the bitter infection you let seep into your heart? When a wound is infected, it doesn't just affect the open area; it spreads and hurts other areas of the body. Suddenly, your whole body is trying to compensate for this one hurt area.

Don't wear your heart down trying to overcompensate for the area where you lost pieces of yourself. Instead, confront the pain.

Try again. Someone is watching who will need to be reminded that you made it and they can, too.

We never know who will be affected by our survival. In the moment, it's hard to see outside of the pain. Only when you dare try to heal will you discover the purpose for your pain.

And, yes, you will have to dare. It may feel uncomfortable at first. You may have to stretch out of your comfort zone. But your blessing is worth the risk. It's worth the pains that come with growth.

Now, more than ever, we have to be brave enough to blaze a trail for one another. May our lives be an example of grace. Remove the facade and admit you're not okay, but you're working to get better. Believe that because of your decision to press forward, future generations will be able to do the same. I know this because Ruth, a woman with a painful past, gave us all a chance for a fruitful future.

Journal

I have a four-year-old daughter named Makenzie Ann. When she was born, her father and I decided to give her my mother's middle name, which means "grace." If you spend enough time with my mother, Makenzie, and me separately, you would be surprised how similarly we act. I have inherited all of the things that I used to fuss at my mother for doing, like being late or procrastinating.

It doesn't just end there, though. Many people tell us the three of us have identical mannerisms, voice inflection, and facial expressions. More often than not, we are interrupted while speaking to be reminded how much we act like one another. When this first started happening, I was frustrated. "I'm my own person," I would tell my siblings, but I continued to think about it.

Everyone who meets my mother feels as though they've had a true encounter with grace. Her very essence embodies humility, kindness, and love. That's not a bad legacy to have passed from generation to generation. Her same compassion can be reflected in the hearts of all of her children; she and I just happen to express it similarly. Her warmth and loving nature have constantly taught us not just to use grace, but to be grace.

If your story ends before the healing, what will the world know about you?

How has your pain hurt the people around you? How has God used it to bless them?

What lesson did you learn through your pain that you hope teaches generations to come?

If your pain saves just one person, it will have served a greater purpose. How can you use your painful past to bless others with a fruitful future?

Prayer

Lord, in the moment, the pain hurts so much I can't imagine how it could help someone else. I just need the strength to endure so that I can tell others about Your grace. I want to turn my wounds into wonders and my pain into purpose. The only way the darkest days of my life can transform into light for someone else is if I realize it's not about me. It's about You! Amen.

30

Collide With Your Destiny

You may have to face the pain of crashing, deal with the memories of what happened, and confront the anxiety of what led you to that moment. You may even be worn down to pieces. But it may be the only way you can collide with your destiny.

Praise be to the Lord, who this day has not left you without a guardian-redeemer."

Ruth 4:14

Recently in Bedford, Virginia, an SUV crashed, causing six passengers to be thrown from the vehicle. The injuries sustained were so extensive that one of the adults and a small child had to be airlifted. The other survivors from the accident were taken by ambulance to the nearest trauma center. All but one were accounted for. A small infant, just a few weeks old, could not be found.

The survivors knew it was unlikely the baby survived. If the impact of the accident didn't kill him, then being thrown out of the vehicle so violently probably did. When the fire department arrived at the scene to determine the quickest way to clean up the debris from the accident, they were also hoping to find the remains of the infant and give the family closure.

What they found stunned everyone. As they lifted the remaining wreckage, they heard the cries of a baby. Trapped under the hood of the large SUV was the car seat the infant had been strapped into at the beginning of the journey. Still secured into the car seat, frightened but unharmed, was the baby they never thought could have survived. From all accounts he should have been dead, permanently injured, or drastically scarred.

Yet somehow the baby was spared.

If someone examined your life and wrote all the details of your collision on paper, others might think your chances of survival were slim to none. Yet here you are. God has spared you and placed your life on reserve.

Your collision was never intended to kill you, so do not let it. Long before your journey began, God strapped you in and promised to protect you from even the most horrific of tragedies. Perhaps at times you stopped trusting Him to see you through and allowed fear to unharness the hold He has on your life. Yet you are still here, and this is proof that He has not given up on you. So you cannot give up on Him.

We've all had our fair share of collisions. There have been moments when it seemed unlikely that we would survive, yet here we are. We may be bruised, but we will keep fighting. We may get burned, but we won't be consumed. We may be afraid, but we won't stop living. We may have to bend, but we will never break.

We don't know why we've had to face so many battles and obstacles in life. There is no true rhyme or reason to why someone like Ruth can be enjoying her life one minute, burying her husband the next, and then leaving her home for a strange land after that. At the time, it must've felt like she was taking one step forward and two steps back. The truth is, she was being pushed out so she could collide head on with destiny. Her plan for her life was good, but God's plan was great.

We have to give up our own desires in order to seek the will of God. When our own plans fail, we cannot become bitter and decide to let go. God is constantly protecting us, even when we face the most awful collisions. Like a small baby unlikely to survive a tragedy, we can make it beyond the pain and arrive at our ultimate purpose.

As broken as we may be, God wants to know we will give Him our all and allow Him to turn our lives into a masterpiece. Countless times Ruth had the opportunity to let the ghost of her past haunt the decisions of her present. We do, too. But I don't want to be controlled by my broken heart or my fear of history repeating itself.

When Ruth's story begins, we see her and Naomi at one of the darkest stages of their lives. When the story ends, their future seems filled with hope, prosperity, and joy. It doesn't mean that future is worry free and without obstacles. It definitely doesn't mean they have arrived at their destination. But they have realized their divine destiny and embraced it. Their story serves as a reminder that it's not about how you start; it's about how you finish.

Who could have guessed that the two broken women we met at the beginning of the story would each find her way back to joy. Different pasts yet similar hurts.

My story may be different from Ruth's, and yours may be different from Naomi's, but neither of our stories has to end where the hurt began. Refuse to bury yourself while there is still air in your lungs. Believe that God is capable of changing your life.

Sometimes the only way to fix a vehicle after an accident is to total it out and get a new one. Even with a new car, you can't change the way you received it. You can't separate the pain from the victory. If you're going to chase after God's best for your life, you must be willing to let your plans be totaled. You may have to face the pain of crashing, deal with the memories of what happened, and confront the anxiety of what led you to that moment. You may even be worn down to pieces. But how else can you collide with your destiny?

The only true way to kill the bitterness of your past is to seek the sweetness of today. There is beauty in struggle. No more than a painter's talent can be judged before she is finished can God's work in our life be judged in the middle of struggle. Don't give up on God because you feel you've been forgotten. You may only see a messy work in progress, but He is creating a masterpiece.

~~~ Journal ~~~

When I first stared writing this book, only a month had passed since my divorce became final. Though we had been separated for quite some time, the actual finality of it all was different. I had not lost hope because I truly believed I did the right thing. The uncertainty was just so scary.

I read the book of Ruth over and over; I truly wanted to know that long before I was born, broken people could still be used. If I could convince myself of this truth, then maybe I could help others, too. But I had to overcome the belief that grace has an expiration date, that the same grace that existed for Ruth couldn't apply to my life today.

Somehow God gave me the crazy courage to open up my life to show that we all need grace. I share the painful truths of my story in my memoir, *Lost and Found*, because sometimes grace needs a face. We need someone who is brave enough to believe that their lives were not over at the point of impact. I share some of my most painful collisions and how I found a piece of myself that I never could have accessed had I not been broken.

It's difficult to trust that all things work together for our good because we can't comprehend how God could do it. If we can't understand it, we don't believe it, and that's how we get cheated into believing in God but not having faith. We must walk on the surface of what threatened to drown us and trust that God will hold us up. It took me a long time to realize this lesson. It's taking me even longer to consistently implement it, but I'm grateful that I'm on the journey to colliding with my destiny.

At what point during the book of Ruth did you realize she was going to learn to live again? What strikes you as the turning point for her collision with destiny?

Where can you see glimpses of your own struggle in her journey?

How did she show God that she could handle more?

How are you showing God that you're strong enough to push past the pain?

Help someone who has been or could be broken in the same way you have been—for example, volunteer at church, mentor others, open communication with family and friends.

Ruth's journey has inspired many, but no one was more inspired than Ruth herself. Do you have what it takes to live an inspired life? What will sustain you?

Prayer

God, I know my life has had many detours. I know that many times I hoped things would go one way and they went another. I didn't mean to make my will more important than Yours. Somehow I just lost myself, trying to find myself. I need the courage to find myself again, but this time I want to find the person You created me to be. I tried it my way. I created an image of what happiness looked like and I lost it all. You are the only One capable of locating my broken pieces and making me whole again. Here I am, God; I need You like never before. Please open my heart so that I can feel, love, and trust again. I want to be the person I was created to be. Please take the wheel and guide me. I'm ready to collide with destiny. Amen.

Sarah Jakes is a businesswoman, writer, speaker, and media personality. She currently oversees the women's ministry at The Potter's House of Dallas, a multicultural, nondenominational church and humanitarian organization led by her parents, Bishop T. D. Jakes and Mrs. Serita Jakes. In addition to her duties at The Potter's House, Sarah periodically serves as host of *The Potter's Touch*, a daily inspirational broadcast airing on several national television networks.

Prior to joining the staff at The Potter's House, Sarah worked with TDJ Enterprises, where she was responsible for grassroots marketing efforts for the feature film *Not Easily Broken*.

After graduating from high school at the age of sixteen in the top 10 of her class and in the top 10 percent of the nation, Sarah attended Texas Christian University, where she studied journalism. She regularly blogs at sarahjakes.com on love, life, family, and marriage and aspires to write articles and books that chronicle the lives of young women who have overcome extreme challenges to reach their goals in life.

When she is not pursuing her career endeavors, Sarah enjoys cooking, listening to music, and spending quality time with her two children.

Don't let your past keep you from a full future.

Like every girl, Sarah Jakes dreamed of a life full of love, laughter, and happy endings. But her dreams changed dramatically when she became pregnant at age thirteen, a reality only compounded by the fact that her father, Bishop T.D. Jakes, was one of the most influential megachurch pastors in the nation. As a teen mom and a high-profile preacher's kid, her road was lonely. She was shunned at school, gossiped about at church. And a few years later, when a fairy-tale marriage ended in a spiral of hurt and rejection, she could have let her pain dictate her future.

Instead, she found herself surrounded by a God she'd given up on, crashing headlong with Him into a destiny she'd never dreamed of. Sarah's captivating story, unflinchingly honest and deeply vulnerable, is a vivid reminder that God can turn even the deepest pain into His perfection.

More than a memoir, *Lost and Found* offers hope and encouragement. Perhaps you, like Sarah, find yourself wandering the detours of life. Regardless of how lost you feel, you, too, can be found.

Lost and Found by Sarah Jakes